William Shakespeare

and His Bible

Also by Dr. I. D. E. Thomas

The Golden Treasury of Puritan Quotations
The Omega Conspiracy
A Day at a Time
Puritan Daily Devotional Chronicles
The Golden Treasury of Patristic Quotations

William Shakespeare and His Bible
© 2000 by I. D. E. Thomas

Printed in the United States of America

Published by
Hearthstone Publishing, Ltd.
P. O. Box 815 ▪ Oklahoma City, OK 73101
405/789-3885 ▪ 888/891-3300 ▪ FAX 405/789-6502

Cover design by Christi Killian
ISBN 1-57558-058-6

William Shakespeare
and His Bible

The Millennium Man

I. D. E. Thomas

Table of Contents

To

MAIR and DAVID

Acknowledgments

It was some years ago that Dr. Noah Hutchings, the vice-president of Hearthstone Publishing, Ltd., casually suggested to me that there should be a book published on Shakespeare's religious convictions. Nothing more was said on the subject, by him or by me.

Soon after my retirement, I read in a British journal that a poll had been conducted in the United Kingdom on the *British Personality of the Millennium*. Shakespeare, the bard of Avon, was ranked Number One. A short time later, a similar poll was conducted in the United States on the *Man of the Millennium*. Shakespeare was ranked Number Five.

These events brought back to mind the suggestion of Dr. Hutchings. Many months of my retirement were then devoted to this one topic: the religious convictions of William Shakespeare.

Now that the book is ready for publication, I want to acknowledge my indebtedness to Dr. Hutchings for his intimation, and also to a number of authors for the books they had written on the life and work of Shakespeare. I read their books ardently, and although not agreeing with every statement in every book, nevertheless I am deeply in their debt for their masterly and scholarly research.

Puritan Profiles by William Barker (Christian Focus Publications, Fearn, Scotland, UK, 1996).

An Inquiry into the Philosophy and Religion of Shakespeare by W. J. Birch, 1848. (Haskell House Publishers, New York, 1972).

A Reader's Guide to Shakespeare by Joseph Rosenblum (Barnes and Noble Books, New York, 1987).

Worldly Saints by Leland Ryken (Zondervan Publishing House, 1986).

Biblical References in Shakespeare's History Plays by Naseeb Shaheen (Newark: University of Delaware Press, 1989).

Shakespeare's Lives by S. Schoenbaum (Clarendon Press, Oxford, 1991).

Alias Shakespeare by Joseph Sobran (The Free Press, New York, 1997).

The Puritan Oligarchy by Thomas Jefferson Wertenbaker (Grosset and Dunlap, New York, 1947).

Tudor Puritanism by Marshall Knappen (Pelican Books, 1949, Harmondsworths, Middlesex, England)

Principles of Shakespearean Production by G. Wilson Knight (Pelican Books, 1836, 1949, Harmondsworths, Middlesex, England).

Makers of Puritan History by Marcus L. Loane (Wm. B. Eerdmans Publishing Co., 1961).

Preface

"Genius" is a word that has been trivialized by overuse in the modern world. But in the classical libraries of the English language, where the masters of literature are placed side by side, few will protest when the word "genius" is used to describe William Shakespeare — as a poet, a playwright, and a dramatist he is without peer.

To fully understand the genius and subtleties of his works, Shakespeare must be set in the context of his time. In the period of his life when he was most prolific, from 1594 to 1608, British society was experiencing upheaval — specifically the Christian religion. And so, the question begs: How could so insightful an observer of human condition fail to have been impacted by the religious disputations of his day? How did they capture his mind and heart? Did he inculcate his personal beliefs into the characters of his masterpieces that speak so eloquently of the frailties of man in every station in life?

Was William Shakespeare in fact a Roman Catholic, caught up, as many were, in a royal spot between Buckingham Palace and the Papal See in Rome? Did he see with his penetrating intellect the feuds, misunderstandings, and tempers in Rome that came vividly to life in the complex characters of his tragedies and comedies? Or, was he sympathetic to the fledgling Church of England? And did those sympathies translate into his many works that dealt with the theme that outward appearances are hardly ever what they seem. Or is there evidence in the four periods of Shakespeare's maturing literary career, that he was also maturing in his Christian faith — influenced by the Puritan movement, which proved so enticing to so many spiritual seekers of his day.

In the first chapter of his book, Dr. Thomas sets the stage — much as Shakespeare would — for the drama that is to unfold. We observe the Puritans — who perhaps founded the term "grassroots politics" — achieving power and influence first in Great Britain and ultimately in the United States.

Then we are led — step by penetrating step — as Dr. Thomas compares Scripture to Shakespeare, including his many references to — and quotes from — John Calvin's Geneva version of Scripture embraced by the Puritans of that period.

Then we arrive at the proof texts of Dr. Thomas' presentation. Weaving together his thorough knowledge of the Bible with his obvious love of and respect for the subtleties of Shakespeare, and the essentials of Puritan theology, the world of dark tragedies and bitter comedies written by William Shakespeare take on an entirely new meaning.

As you complete your journey through this book, Dr. Thomas will leave you at the end with a smile — a smile of satisfaction knowing that the words of Shakespeare in fact reveal him to be not a literary genius, but rather a Christian literary genius.

William Shakespeare and His Bible

The Bard of Stratford-on-Avon had in fact been influenced at a very deep level by a maturing faith that flowed from his heart and from his mind, through his characters and their thoughts, motivations, actions, and words, and into the greatest English literature the world has ever known.

To appreciate his genius best, we learn the delicate touch the genius used to bring his deeply held faith to life in works that will be read, analyzed, and enjoyed forever.

—Warren Duffy

Introduction

What was the religion of Shakespeare? Was he a Roman Catholic, an Episcopalian, or a Puritan? Books have been written on all three.

Some have agreed with Thomas Carter, a Presbyterian minister, who wrote a book in 1897, *Shakespeare, Puritan and Recusant.*

Some have agreed with Richard Simpson and Henry G. Bowden, who in their book *The Religion of Shakespeare*, written in 1899, claimed that he belonged to the Old Faith, the term often used in England at the time for the Roman Catholic Faith.

Others, probably the vast majority, claim that Shakespeare was an Anglican/Episcopalian. That was the Established Church of England, and their church in Stratford-upon-Avon was called Holy Trinity Church. It was there that William Shakespeare was christened, it was there that he became a member, it was there that he was later appointed a lay-rector, and it was there, inside the church, that he was buried.

With the historical information at our disposal, it is incredible that a few authors, who have written extensively on Shakespeare's life and works, have dismissed his whole religious experience with one tiny, cursory sentence, "he was a catholic." They are undoubtedly experts in the literary field, but apparently amateurs in the religious field.

The purpose of this book is to take another look at Shakespeare's religious convictions. Recognizing that he was officially a member of the Established Church of England (Episcopalian), we also believe that deep down he shared in some of the Puritan doctrines and principles of that era. It was not an unusual thing in the England of the seventeenth century; and many noted personalities, divines and laity, adopted that position. They were members of the Established Church *without conforming.*

How strong then was Shakespeare's Puritan learning and leaning? Some of the evidence presented in this book will be circumstantial, dealing with Shakespeare's family and friends, his ministers and mentors, particularly after his return to Stratford to retire. Other evidence we will attempt to garner from Shakespeare's own writings, especially the plays he authored. Like most people in England at that time, he probably believed in the "Divine Rights of Kings," and probably went further than that, believing in the "crown rights of the Redeemer," and again growing from that, in the Puritan principle of the divine right of the liberty of conscience. Soon, it became referred to as the inviolable rights of free peoples.

Some have claimed that Shakespeare's works do not reveal a single trace of his own personal beliefs. That conclusion we find difficult to accept, knowing that Shakespeare lived through a time of great spiritual turmoil in Britain, what Hazlitt called "a mighty fermentation." It is impossible to believe that a man of Shakespeare's stature and ingenuity could remain aloof from the chaos that swirled around him. How could he not reveal a trace of what was happening to the religion he had been raised in? With the conflict raging between the Old Faith and the New Faith, how could the literary genius from Stratford remain completely unconcerned?

In spite of the claim that his plays tell us nothing about Shakespeare's personal beliefs, many of those who have made a recondite study on the matter have come to a different conclusion. They may not all agree on the minutiae, but they do agree that here and there in his plays, there are indications of what Shakespeare believed about "the faith which was once delivered to the saints." The *dramatis personae* will naturally present different viewpoints and lifestyles, but underneath it all, many have been able to detect the undertone of the great author himself.

Puritanism in Shakespeare's Day

(1564-1616)

1 Most people have a fairly good idea as what it means to be a Roman Catholic; a little fewer would be as conversant with the term Episcopalian, or as it is known to many, Anglican; but fewer still would be able to explain what it means to be a Puritan.

It may be appropriate to begin at that very point: what exactly do we mean by the term Puritanism? In our schools and colleges we have been taught very little about our own Puritan heritage. It reminds us of one of Sherlock Holmes' mysteries, where the key to solving a case was the fact that when a man was murdered a certain dog didn't bark! Someone called it *the presence of an absence!* There is an absence in many of us today, an absence of knowledge regarding our great Christian heritage, particularly our Puritan heritage. This, in spite of the wealth of Puritan literature at our disposal.

What then do we know about Puritanism, and what did Shakespeare know about it? There are two major views, contrary views, as to what Puritanism actually was. One view could be represented in a statement made by H. L. Mencken: "The haunting fear that someone, somewhere, may be happy." The other view as expressed by F. N. Macauley: the Puritans were "perhaps the most remarkable body of men which the world has ever produced."

These two viewpoints still persist. In many countries, the Puritans have received bad press. Much of the time their image in the media has been caustic. The Puritan has been cast as a sour, dour killjoy, and often as an uncultured Philistine. Others still believe that the Puritans, when rightly understood, were the arbiters of public purity and character.

It is of interest that the word *Puritan* did not appear in our language until the year 1564, which happened to be the year that Shakespeare was born!

History informs us that the Puritans were convinced that the Protestant Reformation in England had been stunted. It was never allowed to proceed to its logical conclusion. The first generation of Puritans tried to bring about necessary reforms by *political action*. However, they were no match to Queen Elizabeth I, and they were politically defeated.

Having failed to reform the church by political action from the top down, they sought to do so by *persuasion* from the bottom up. To this end, they used pulpit, press, pamphlets, and books, plus moral persuasion. In the next century, they did achieve political power, and Oliver Cromwell became Lord Protector of England.

There is no question but that the Puritans exercised great influence on the United Kingdom. When the exiles returned from the continent, they brought with them the doctrines of John Calvin, plus the English Bible, the **Geneva Version,** which they had produced.

In time, the Puritans exercised an even greater influence on the United States of America. One of America's leading historians, Bancroft, claimed that Calvin was "the Father of America." In the present time, Rabbi Marc H. Tannenbaum claims that,

> Not to understand Puritanism is not to understand America. Like the Hebrews, the Puritans looked upon themselves as God's chosen people, comparing their New England states to those of the ancient Israelites. . . . For both Hebrews and Puritans, God was the only true monarch.

In the United Kingdom, the king had supreme power. They referred to it as "the Divine Rights of Kings." REX is LEX. A Scottish Puritan, Samuel Rutherford, then wrote a book which he entitled *LEX Is REX.* This was the position adopted by the United States, not that the *king* is *law,* but that *law* is *king!* As portrayed in the American Constitution, every man, whether living in the White House or in a house on Skid Row, is subject to the law.

An outstanding distinctive of the Puritan was his massive, intellectual capacity. This was equaled only by the profundity of his spiritual comprehension, and the totality of his dedication to God. No men ever were more conversant with the whole sweep of biblical revelation, or more specialized in the probing and discerning of human behavior. As seers of Divine truth and as surgeons of human souls, the Puritans remain peerless.

William Shakespeare and His Bible

In their day, many of the Puritans belonged to the more educated class of their society. They abounded in the universities, and supplied some of their most distinguished scholars. For one period of time, the great majority in the English Parliament were Puritans.

It has been claimed that the Puritans brought a spiritual light to England, and stamped a moral greatness upon her, more than any other group had done, before or after. Grounded in biblical truth, they were uncompromising in their condemnation of moral declension, political unrighteousness, and religious apostasy.

Dr. Lorraine Boettner claimed that Cromwell's army "for purity and heroism surpassed anything the world has ever seen."

And Professor John Fiske, ranked as one of the two greatest American historians, asserts:

> It is not too much to say that in the seventeenth century the entire political future of mankind was staked upon the questions that were at issue in England. Had it not been for the Puritans, political liberty would probably have disappeared from the world. If ever there were men who laid down their lives in the cause of all mankind, it was those grim old Ironsides, whose watch-words were texts of Holy Writ, whose battle cries were hymns of praise.

Some claim that although the Puritans did produce some great theological tomes and sermon volumes, they never produced any great religious or ecclesiastical paintings, architecture, sculpture, or even music. Such critics forget, however, that the Puritans were represented in the higher literature of the Elizabethan period. Many of them expressed in their literature both the Puritan doctrine and the Puritan spirit. One immediately thinks of men like *John Milton, John Bunyan,* and *Edmund Spenser.*

It was Spenser who wrote *The Shepherd's Calendar,* and also *The Faery Queen* — the word *faery* meaning *spiritual.* The historian Green stated that this great poet, often referred to as the poets' poet, "strikes the note of the coming Puritanism." The same historian said of John Milton that he was "not only the highest but the completest type of Puritan." And another great historian, Macauley, was so indebted to Bunyan that he claimed regarding his book *Pilgrim's Progress* that

> there is no book in our literature on which we would so readily stake the fame of the old, unpolluted English language, no book which shows so well how rich that language is in its own proper wealth, and how little it has been improved by all that it has borrowed.

Today, Spenser's *The Faery Queen*, Bunyan's *Pilgrim's Progress,* and Milton's *Paradise Lost,* are our gateway into the world of English Puritanism.

Of interest to many, however, is the question: what about another author, playwright, and poet, often said to be of greater imperial intellect than any author in English history, **William Shakespeare**? If the Puritan hurricane was able to sway the mind and zest of authors of the prestige of Milton, Spenser, and Bunyan, why not an author of even greater prestige, the bard of Avon?

It may be advisable to remind ourselves of what G. Wilson Knight wrote in 1936 in *Principles of Shakespearean Production.* He tells us that most people deny that Shakespeare was a religious poet, but this is not so. Great poems by Dante and Milton are able to blame the human and the Divine. ". . . Those poets who aim primarily to speak of God do so in terms of man; and Shakespeare, speaking with the accents and intricacies of great poetry of man, speaks accordingly of God." Knight describes Shakespeare as "a man of spiritual sensibility with a keen and able mind."

❖ ❖ ❖ ❖ ❖

In 1999 a poll was conducted in the United Kingdom on the *British Personality of the Millennium.* Churchill came in second, Darwin came in fourth, with others like Queen Elizabeth I and Margaret Thatcher on the list. But Number One on that list was the bard of Avon, *William Shakespeare.* It is interesting that even in America's *Men of the Millennium,* Shakespeare ranked Number Five.

This is not that surprising when we recall that a man like the German Goethe called him a "heavenly genius." And the French Andre Gide, when asked who was France's greatest poet, answered, "Hugo, alas." "He was not disparaging Victor Hugo," said Joseph Sobran, "but lamenting that there had been no French Shakespeare."

❖ ❖ ❖ ❖ ❖

There is one fact, however, that still remains a mystery. In spite of all his plays and poems, Shakespeare himself remains very much in the shadows. In another quotation from Sobran, we are told that "after four centuries, Shakespeare remains the most haunting of authors. He seems to know us better than we know him."

What we do know about him with certainty, is that he was born in Stratford-upon-Avon in the year 1564. By today's standards, Stratford was a small town of about twelve hundred population. The largest city in England, outside of London, was Norwich, and it had less than fifteen thousand people. They were all small towns in those days. Liverpool had only a thousand people. Most people in the days of Shakespeare lived in small, scattered villages.

We know that in 1582 Shakespeare married Anne Hathaway and had three children with her: Susanna, and twins Hamnet and Judith. Very little else has been written about his personal, private life.

He became famous when he began writing. He wrote many poems and thirty-seven plays. None of the thirty-seven were published until 1623, seven years after his death. This great collection was called **The First Folio.**

❖ ❖ ❖ ❖ ❖

Some scholars claim that the best writers of English are those who knew other languages also. Shakespeare falls into that category, being that he also knew Latin and French. Sobran is convinced that the real threat to English today is not foreign languages, but the reduction of English "to a few functional grunts." He accuses some of our current leaders of not being able to say anything memorable, or even remember memorable things!

Maybe, contributing to that factor, is another factor, namely, that two-thirds of our top universities no longer insist that English majors take a Shakespeare course. By so doing, they are ignoring the greatest author in the English language, the man who has been referred to as the "master spirit of the world of letters."

At a time, however, when academia is ignoring our great cultural inheritance, Shakespeare is not only surviving, but thriving on our college campuses. We read in some of our newspapers and journals that elective classes devoted to the bard of Avon are bulging at the seams. Dr. Samuel Johnson was correct when he said, back in 1765, that "people read Shakespeare because they want to, not because they have to."

C. S. Lewis, who was himself a noted Oxford lecturer and Christian author, was highly knowledgeable in both our Puritan and literary heritage. He used to advise his students to read one old book for every contemporary book they read, not because those authors were always right, but because they at least made different mistakes from our contemporaries!

❖ ❖ ❖ ❖ ❖

It is claimed that about 750 million people speak English today (375 million as their first language, and another 375 million as their second language.) It was said on the BBC about a dozen years ago, that

William Shakespeare and His Bible

in the days of Shakespeare the number who spoke English was less than seven million! The number grew rapidly, however, and part of the credit for that is given to Shakespeare.

H. L. Mencken, in his book *The American Language,* tells us that in Shakespeare's day, Englishmen were free "to mold their language to the throng of new ideas, that naturally marked an era of adventure and expansion." He added also that "Shakespeare himself either invented or introduced to good literary society" a large number of new words. Even Thomas Gray had to admit that both Shakespeare and Milton had enriched the English language with "words of their own composition or invention." And in our day, Harold Bloom, a professor at Yale University, tells us that "early modern English was shaped by Shakespeare: the Oxford English Dictionary is made in his image."

Today, those who speak English often quote Shakespeare without even knowing it! We quote him when we use such common expressions as:

fast and loose	a tower of strength
tongue tied	cold comfort
in a pickle	salad days
kill with kindness	the game is up
ill-starred	a laughing stock
bare-faced	the devil incarnate
hunch-backed	the naked truth
your teeth set on edge	

Phrases from Shakespeare's plays have become everyday expressions:

⋄ I have not slept one wink — *Cymbeline*

- We have seen better days — *As You Like It*
- The short and the long of it — *The Merry Wives of Windsor*
- Neither rhyme nor reason — *The Comedy of Errors*
- Dead as a doornail — *Henry VI*
- It was Greek to me — *Julius Caesar*
- I'll not budge an inch — *The Taming of the Shrew*
- Fool's paradise — *Romeo and Juliet*
- Give the devil his due — *Henry IV*
- The course of true love never did run smooth — *Midsummer Night's Dream*
- It is a wise father that knows his own child — *The Merchant of Venice*

All the following, and more, come from one play, *Hamlet:*

- More in sorrow than anger
- The time is out of joint
- Brevity is the soul of wit
- I must be cruel only to be kind
- Though this be madness, yet there is method in it
- A king of shreds and patches
- The rest is silence

❖ ❖ ❖ ❖ ❖

As we know, there has been endless controversy as to whom Shakespeare really was. Many claim that his name has been an *alias* for someone else. Names like Francis Bacon, Edward de Vere, Christopher Marlowe, and others have been suggested. The majority of people, however, are of the opinion that those who question the fact that Shakespeare was the actual author must be eccentrics or cranks! They feel it is plain snobbery to suggest that a man of modest origin and education could not have become the outstanding genius of English literature. As Louis B. Wright tells us, such people forget that "genius has a way of cropping up in unexpected places, and that none of the great creative writers of the world got his inspiration in a college or university course."

On one point, however, there is no debate. Whoever Shakespeare *was,* we all know *what he was.* He remains, after four centuries, the most phenomenal author of the English-speaking world.

Ben Johnson, a contemporary of Shakespeare and himself an eminent writer of the Elizabethan era, was sometimes critical of Shakespeare. On one occasion when the actors of London wanted to honor Shakespeare, they said : "Whatsoever he penned, he never blotted out a line." Jonson answered: "Would he had blotted out a thousand!" In his final testimony to Shakespeare, however, he described him as "honest, and of an open and free nature; he had an excellent fancy, brave notions, and gentle expressions . . . he redeemed his vices with his virtues. There was ever more in him to be praised than to be pardoned."

Four hundred years later, Shakespeare is being described as our cultural icon. Some years ago Harold Bloom referred to Shakespeare as "the Western canon," only to be superseded later by another Bloom blast:

Shakespeare is not only in himself the Western canon, but has become *the universal canon,* perhaps the only one that can survive the current debasement of our teaching institutions. Every other great writer may fall away, to be replaced by the anti-elitist swamp of Cultural Studies. Shakespeare will abide, even if he were to be expelled by the academics. . . .

And who can dispute the judgment of the premier poet of Puritanism, John Milton, in his brilliant epitaph "On Shakespeare 1630":

Thou in our wonder and astonishment
Hast built thy self a live-long Monument

....

And so Sepulcher'd in such pomp dost lie,
That Kings for such a Tomb would wish to die.

His Family and Friends

2 Regarding **John Shakespeare,** his father, some claim that he was a closet Catholic; others that he was an Episcopalian; and still others that he was a Puritan, and a very strong Puritan.

Like his son William, John Shakespeare certainly lived in a time when doctrinal controversies were tearing the fabric of society. People often had to camouflage their true religious beliefs. It was the *in-thing* for people to exercise caution in expressing their religious faith.

During the reign of Queen Mary, an inflexible Roman Catholic, heresy trials were the order of the day. All around Stratford there had been a circle of martyr fires, particularly in Coventry, Lichfield, Gloucester, Banbury, and Oxford. Women as well as men were burned at the stake. In Coventry, a woman gave birth when she was being burned, and the baby was immediately thrown back on to the burning faggots. Queen Mary soon became known throughout England as "Bloody Mary." At one point, the famous Scottish preacher John Knox wrote a letter, more like a manifesto, to the "professors of God's truth in

England," stating that Queen Mary was more blood-thirsty than Jezebel.

Queen Mary had come to the throne in 1553, two years after John Shakespeare had moved to Stratford. In 1555, Latimer and Ridley were burnt at the stake in Oxford, and a year later, Archbishop Cranmer met the same fate. The Roman Catholic faith had once more become the established religion of the realm.

John Shakespeare, although born a Protestant, now, according to some, became a Roman Catholic, and he was sometimes referred to as a closet Catholic. Because of the confusion that existed at that time, and the endless controversies, religion to many became, as Thomas Carter tells us, "a matter of convenience and not conviction." This may be the reason why some claim that William Shakespeare was raised in a Roman Catholic home.

There is no documentary evidence, however, to prove that. There is far more evidence to prove that the family was associated with the Episcopalian or Anglican church in Stratford, namely, the Holy Trinity Church. It was there that William Shakespeare was christened, and it was there, fifty-two years later, that he was buried.

After the death of Queen Mary, Elizabeth I became queen. Things changed drastically, especially in matters concerning religion. Queen Elizabeth I was a Protestant, and soon a new law was passed commissioning the destruction of all Roman Catholic "Altars, Crosses, and Vaine Symbols."

At that time, John Shakespeare was the chief magistrate and bailiff of the city of Stratford, a position similar to that of mayor in our day, and thus had a vital role in seeing that the queen's law was carried out. In 1564, the year that William was born, John Shakespeare saw to it that the old chapel that used to be Roman Catholic was altered to conform with the new religious trend in England. All Roman Catholic emblems were torn down or defaced and, according to Dugdale, it was done *in a thoroughly Puritan spirit*. Needless to say, if John Shakespeare had himself been a true Catholic, he would never have assumed such a prominent role in defacing and mutilating his own church.

In a book published a little over a hundred years ago, under the title *Shakespeare, Puritan and Recusant*, Thomas Carter has no hesitation in referring to John Shakespeare as a Puritan, and that he had engaged not only in defacing images, but also in selling the ecclesiastical vestments as well. The Puritans referred to this as "the last relics of the Amorites." There is also evidence that in 1572 when great efforts were made in Parliament to favor reforms of the church, John Shakespeare was one of the three delegates appointed by the city of Stratford to go to London in order to further the said reform.

When Queen Elizabeth I ascended the throne, she needed all the Puritan support she could get because of strong Roman Catholic reaction in the north of England, and also on the continent of Europe, particularly in Spain and France. Some years later, however, the queen felt that the Puritans in England were getting too numerous and too powerful. Not only had they gained in popularity, but even the universities were becoming Puritan to the core. In view of this, the queen instigated certain repressive measures in order to curb, if not to crush, the

Puritan movement.

At this time, life became difficult for many Puritans. Even Grindal, the Archbishop of Canterbury, by order of the Star Chamber, was confined to his residence and sequestered from his functions. Many Puritans, especially in the Warwick area, were persecuted and imprisoned. The queen explained her actions, clearer than any journalist or historian, when she told the French ambassador that "she would maintain the religion she was crowned in and baptized in, and would suppress the papistical religion, that it should not grow; but that she would root out Puritanism and the favourers thereof."

Subsequent history proved that the queen meant what she said. It is true that many Catholics had paid a high price for their faith; now, persecution of non-conforming Puritans began. Very soon they were filling the dungeons and graves of England. An act of Parliament was passed, with the full authority of the queen, to punish "persons obstinately refusing to come to Church and persuading others to impugn the Queen's authority in Ecclesiastical causes." Her commissioners had "the powers of perpetual imprisonment, perpetual banishment, *and death without benefit of clergy.*" That latter privilege was one that the vilest felon could always claim, but now the Puritan prisoner was denied even that.

The Puritans who had felt the favor and now the fury of the queen, understood more clearly what their Savior had endured. One day the crowds praised Him with their shouts of "Hosanna to the Son of David," and a little later they persecuted Him, shouting, "Let him be crucified. . . . His blood be upon us." In Shakespeare's play *Timon of Athens,* one of the characters says:

> *I should fear those that dance before me now*
> *would one day stamp upon me. 'T'as been done.*
> *Men shut their doors against a setting sun.*

The persecution of the Puritans, said Carter, caused many Englishmen "to gaze with wistful longing across the wild waves of the Atlantic to where the New World offered religious freedom and liberty of conscience."

It never dawned on the queen of England that the Puritan principles that she deplored would in time sweep from land to land, and instead of the "Divine Rights of Kings," men would proclaim the "Divine rights of conscience."

Many are of the opinion that it was at that time that John Shakespeare was becoming more of a Puritan than an Episcopalian. There is evidence that in 1592 he was heavily fined for failing to attend the parish church in Stratford. There were two opinions given as to why he absented himself. Some believed that he was financially deprived at the time and heavily in debt. By not attending the parish church, he would avoid having to meet the people to whom he was indebted! A much more plausible opinion is that he was attending a Christian service in nearby Warwick, where the famous Puritan preacher Thomas Cartwright was drawing large crowds. This was only a few miles from Shakespeare's home, and many believed that it is there that you would find John Shakespeare on Sunday mornings.

One could add another event to the life of John Shakespeare that would imply very forcibly that he had Puritan tendencies. When the queen had to quell a Roman Catholic uprising in the north of England, John Shakespeare was the leading figure on the Stratford town council. He appealed to all the citizens of Stratford to give the queen their full support. Some time later, however, when the same queen tried to suppress the Puritans because they expressed disapproval of some of her policies, John Shakespeare took no part whatsoever. By his refusal to comply with the queen's request, he was open to all the penalties of noncompliance. It was obvious that by then John Shakespeare had close ties with the Puritan movement.

Thomas Carter stated the same conclusion in his book, when he said that from the moment the queen began suppressing the Puritans, John Shakespeare took very little part in the activities of the Stratford town council. He writes:

> It is instructive to note the change that comes over his political and civic activity when the Puritan is being harried throughout the land. He avoids all legal controversies, ceases to attend the Council meetings, and finally allows his name to be struck off the rolls as an alderman.

Some believe that we will never know the full answers to all these questions about John Shakespeare. Be that as it may, we still have sufficient information from both circumstantial and documentary evidence, that John Shakespeare had strong Puritan leanings, in both doctrine and practice.

He was undoubtedly a member of the Anglican Church of Stratford, known as the Holy Trinity

Church. However, there is another fact we must realize, that in those days in England, many of the Puritans, clergy and laity, were members of the Established Church, i.e. the Anglican or Episcopalian Church. In this sense, as one author puts it, John Shakespeare was a Prelatist and a Puritan.

Knowing all this, we can be confident that when William Shakespeare was a young boy at home, he was taught the Bible daily and became acquainted with Divine truth. There is no doubt that it was John Shakespeare who played the major role in this, but there is also evidence that his mother, Anne Shakespeare, had a vital role as well. In his earlier years, she would teach him the lessons of piety and a reverence for the Holy Bible. Throughout the land at that time, people considered the Bible to be the "Book of Books."

In addition to knowing the Bible, young William would also have been taught how to pray. At meal times in the England of the Tudor era, no child would dare touch his knife, spoon, trencher, or plate, without first participating in a lengthy grace. In this way the children soon learned how to pray themselves. Much of the conversation around the table would be about stories from the Bible. Often their humor would come from the Bible, plus endless questions, and sometimes trick questions. A child would be asked: "Who killed the fourth part of all people in the world?" And the answer would be: "Cain, when he killed Abel."

Part of the home regime also, was to make sure that the children were taught to respect and obey their father. William Shakespeare referred to it later as "domestic awe."

It is interesting that in one of his plays, (*The Merchant of Venice*) we find this sentence: "*To you, your father should be as a god.*"

We should ask at this point, when John Shakespeare taught the Bible to his family in Stratford, what sort of a Bible did he use?

❖ ❖ ❖ ❖ ❖

We know for certain that young William Shakespeare was taught more of the Bible at home than anywhere else. Years later, when he wrote his plays in London, no brilliance of intellect could have made him quote so copiously from the Bible, and quote with such indisputable accuracy, unless he had from his early years at home been trained and steeped in Bible study.

Thomas Carter was convinced that if Shakespeare had spent the whole of his first twelve years in London in exclusive study of the Bible, "it is questionable if even then he could have attained the perfect ease of quotation he manifests." One thus has to conclude that for this and other reasons, William Shakespeare received most of his Bible learning in his home in Stratford.

To ascertain what Bible they used in that home is very easy. If it had been a Roman Catholic home, and his father a member of the Catholic church, William Shakespeare's Bible quotations would have been from the Vulgate, the Roman Catholic Bible. The Vulgate was written in Latin, and he would have had to translate it himself into English. The Roman Catholic Bible in English, known as the Douai Bible, did not appear until 1609, when practically all of

Shakespeare's plays had already been written.

It is quite obvious that the Bible used in Shakespeare's home in Stratford was written in the vernacular tongue, English. And we also know from the numerous Bible quotations in his plays that it was the Puritan Bible, often known as the *Geneva Version.*

We also know from history that in the England of Shakespeare's day, any Roman Catholic who possessed a Bible in the vulgar tongue was transgressing the rules of the Roman Catholic Church. To possess such a Bible, let alone teach it, was prohibited by the church. Even as late as 1816, Pope Pius VII issued a Bull against Bible societies, making it clear that "the Bible printed by heretics is to be numbered among other prohibited books, for it is evident from experience that the Holy Scriptures, when circulated in the vulgar tongue have, through the temerity of men, produced more harm than benefit." And a Catholic priest, even later than that, remarked publicly that "he would rather a Catholic should read the worst works of immorality than the Protestant Bible, that forgery of God's Word."

We can thus firmly conclude that if John Shakespeare participated in the reform of the church, in defacing Roman Catholic images and emblems, and instructed his family in the Puritan Bible . . . then William Shakespeare was not raised as a Roman Catholic.

❖ ❖ ❖ ❖ ❖

During young William's education at the Stratford grammar school, no doubt the greatest influence on him there would have been that of his headmaster, **Thomas Hunt.**

William was under the discipline and tutelage of Thomas Hunt for five years, between the ages of eight and thirteen. Thomas Hunt was a Puritan, and a strong Puritan. He later became the curate of All Saints' Church in Luddington, but was ultimately deprived of his church vocation because of his Puritan leanings.

As a schoolmaster in Stratford, Thomas Hunt was more qualified than most to teach the Bible to his students. William Shakespeare happened to be one of those students.

There are some who have claimed that William's learning was not that much! "A little Latin and less Greek," said Ben Jonson. Whilst recognizing the possibility of that being true, a Mrs. Griffith wrote very appropriately in her book, *The Morality of Shakespeare's Drama,* that "it would be an invidious reflection on our poet's fame to suppose him to have been a scholar. A genius leads thoughts, a scholar but borrows them."

No one can deny, of course, that William, like most students, was not entirely free from the levities and indiscretions of youth, but neither can they deny that his education had a consequential influence on his character, particularly his spiritual character. The copious scriptural references found throughout his plays indicate clearly that he had been well-grounded in Bible knowledge. As more than one author has testified, Shakespeare was saturated with the Word of God.

It is easy then to conclude from these unequivocal facts that the Puritan teacher and the Puritan

Bible played a prominent role in molding the thoughts and concepts of William Shakespeare in the Puritan tradition.

Comparisons have often been made between two of Europe's greatest authors, Dante, the Italian poet, and Shakespeare, the English poet and playwright. One was a papist, and the other, we believe, a Puritan. Both of them, however, shared one thing in common: a systematic, religious training in their childhood years.

Father Bowden said of Dante, that "in politics, philosophy, and theology, Dante is essentially Catholic and orthodox." He went on to say that in addition to the Bible, Dante drew his most precious material from theology and from the revelations of the saints, *and constantly turned to the "Church's liturgy and office as his most fitting expression."*

This, undoubtedly, was the main difference in the religious training of the two. Shakespeare, the Puritan, would turn instinctively not to church liturgy and office, but to the Holy Bible, as he did consistently throughout his life.

Whatever influences he encountered in London, there is no doubt that in his upbringing in Stratford, at home, at school, and at church, he was well grounded in biblical and Puritan principles.

❖ ❖ ❖ ❖ ❖

As one reads the life story of William Shakespeare, it is evident that of his three children, his favorite was **Susanna.**

The name Susanna may not have been all that familiar in Stratford, but it was the name chosen by

William and Anne Shakespeare. It also happened to be a name much favored by the Puritans, primarily because of its biblical linkage. By the time of Shakespeare, the Puritans were already encouraging their people not to use names associated with Roman Catholic saints in post-apostolic times. This was the time when some of the die-hard Puritans were unhappy with words like *Christmas,* because it reminded them of the Roman Catholic *mass.* One suggested changing Christ*mas* to Christ-*tide*!

Like every other movement, before and after, Puritanism had its radical fringes. One Puritan went so far as to suggest doing away with the term *saint,* and to substitute *sir!* Instead of St. Peter and St. Paul, Sir Peter and Sir Paul! Even Sir Mary!

The vast majority of Puritans, however, were far wiser not only in their doctrines, but in their terminologies. They took the advice of John Knox, who in his *Book of Discipline,* written in 1560, told them: "Let persuasions be used that such names that do not savor of either paganism or popery be given to children at their baptism, but principally those whereof there are examples in the Scriptures."

The name Susanna actually comes from the Apocrypha, which, of course, was included in the Puritan Bible. Susanna was the virtuous wife of Joachim, and lived in accordance with the Mosaic Law. William and Anne Shakespeare, knowing that their daughter had been conceived out of wedlock, revealed a little defiance in their choice of the name Susanna. The name actually asserted *purity* and *spiritual strength.*

In the Apocrypha, the virtuous Susanna had been trapped by two lustful judges. Her screams attracted attention, and servants soon came to her rescue. In court the next day, the judges saw to it that Susanna was condemned as an adulteress. However, God sent a young Daniel to her aid, and he was able to make the two judges contradict each other. The end result was that the two judges were put to death, and Susanna and her family praised God for her deliverance.

❖ ❖ ❖ ❖ ❖

When Susanna Shakespeare became a young woman, she married **John Hall,** a noted physician in Stratford. John Hall was himself a Puritan, and according to some reports, as well known for his theology as for his medicine! They were married in Holy Trinity Church, with her father, William Shakespeare, giving away the bride. When the minister asked: "Who giveth this woman to be married to this man?" Shakespeare then relinquished the bride, and his role in Susanna's life would be ended. He entrusted his favorite daughter to her Puritan husband. Sometime later, Susanna gave birth to her only child, and William Shakespeare became a grandfather at forty-three.

As stated already, Susanna was her father's favorite child, and in his will he left most of his property to her and her heirs. He also made Susanna executor of his will, and her husband John Hall as co-executor.

From the records available, John Hall was a devoted member of Holy Trinity Church in Stratford, and it was he who presented the church with their new, well-carved pulpit. That same pulpit served the church for over a century. In 1628, John Hall was made the Church Warden of Holy Trinity Church. More than one report tells us that John Hall became a very close friend of a number of prominent Puritan divines, especially John Trapp and Thomas Watson.

If further proof was necessary regarding his religious and Puritan character, one should read in Thomas Carter's book about his recovery from a deadly fever. In it we are told of John Hall's "Prayer of Thanksgiving:"

> Thou, O Lord, which hast the power of life and death and drawest from the gates of death, I confess without any art or counsel of man but only from Thy goodness and clemency. Thou hast saved me from the bitter and deadly symptoms of a deadly fever, beyond the expectation of all about me, restoring me as it were from the very jaws of death to former health, for which I praise Thy name, O most Merciful God and Father of our Lord Jesus Christ. . . .

❖ ❖ ❖ ❖ ❖

When Shakespeare died on April 23, 1616, he was buried *inside* the Holy Trinity Church in Stratford — inside the church not because of his fame as a playwright and poet, but because during the last seven or eight years of his life he was a *lay-rector.* By doing so, Poet's Corner in Westminster Abbey, London, was robbed of their greatest prize.

His Ministers and Mentors

3 Some people still believe that William Shakespeare at heart was a Catholic. The fact that he seemed indifferent to church reforms suggests to them that he was of the Old Faith. Having explained already the position adopted by his father and members of his family, and the fact that he was not only a member but a lay-rector of the Anglican/Episcopalian church in Stratford, plus the evidence we will produce from his own plays, should make it extremely difficult for anyone to believe with any degree of certainty that Shakespeare was a member of the Roman Catholic Church. Those who still do so are just conveying an argument from silence. Even W. J. Birch, who considered Shakespeare to be an irreligious man, does admit this one thing:

> Shakespeare, different from the rest of the brother dramatists, did not die in harness; we hear of him in his retirement at Stratford-upon-Avon. There, if anywhere, in the country, a pro-

vincial town, apart from his profession, and friends, and from metropolitan influences, he might have retired, like the Duke in *As You Like It,* put on a religious life, and thrown into neglect the pomps and vanities of this world.

The vast majority undoubtedly concede that William Shakespeare was an Anglican/Episcopalian. Our own conclusion, after a study of his background and upbringing, his life and his work, is that he was an Episcopalian *with a difference.* And he was not alone in that. As a matter of fact, thousands upon thousands of people living in England at that time were in the identical mold that Shakespeare was in. That mold was the Puritan mold, consisting of some of the highest parliamentarians, university professors, preachers and pastors, and even some of the nobility themselves. They were members of the Established Church of England, but, in spite of that, embraced the doctrines and principles of the Puritans.

The one thing that makes it difficult for many people to believe that Shakespeare could be a Puritan was the fact that he was a playwright and an actor. Puritanism, they argue, was against the theater, and nothing could please them more than seeing all the theaters closed.

There is, of course, a lot of truth in that argument. Shakespeare did write for and act in the theater. He even had his own company in London and built their own theater, the Globe. He obviously encouraged and participated in an art form that was repugnant to many Puritans. Most Puritans were of the opinion that nothing could kindle the fire of lust in young people than to frequent stage plays.

One Puritan wrote that "horrible enormities and swelling sins were shown on the stage, with their glittering costumes, and men dressed as women." Another Puritan referred to the theater as a sink of "theft and whoredom, pride and prodigality, villainy and blasphemy." And still another stated that "whosoever shall visit the chapel of Satan, I mean the theater, shall find there no want of young ruffians."

When Shakespeare was twenty-three, a book was published in London, which described actors as *fiends,* "sent from their great captain Satan to deceive the world. . . ." It went on to describe them further as *apes, hell hounds, vipers, painted sepulchers, dogs, caterpillars.* The title of the book was *A Mirror of Monsters.*

This was the time when Philip Stubbs was distributing his book, entitled *Anatomy of Abuses,* referring to the theaters as "Satan's synagogues." The book went on to say:

> If you will learn to play the vice, to swear, tear, and blaspheme both Heaven and Earth; if you would learn to become a bawd, unclean, and to devirginate maids, to deflower honest wives; if you will learn to murder, flay, kill, pick, steal, rob, and row. . . . If you will learn to play the whore-master, the glutton, drunkard, or incestuous person; if you will learn to become proud, haughty, and arrogant; and, finally, if you will learn to condemn God and all his laws, to care neither for heaven nor hell, and to commit all kinds of sin and mischief, you need to go to no other school, for all these good examples may you see painted before your eyes in interludes and plays.

It has been suggested by one modern author, that if this tirade by Stubbs was modernized and polished a little, it would be an apt description of the evils perpetrated by modern-day Hollywood!

❖ ❖ ❖ ❖ ❖

To present the whole picture, one should state that the Puritans were not alone in their condemnation of much that was happening in the theaters of London at that time. They received a lot of support from the London Council, not only because of the profanity heard on many of the stages, but they also felt that whenever a large crowd came together, they could very well plot sedition. The only large crowd the councillors felt safe with, was a crowd listening to a sermon! In view of this, the London Council passed an ordinance that no theater performance could be given in London on Sundays, or on any other holy day. It should be added that it was not only the London councillors, but some of the high church bishops, members of the royal family, and other municipalities expressed the same view.

In time, as we know, the Puritan movement gathered sufficient force to close the theaters of London completely for twenty years. In the words of W. J. Birch: "The Bacons and the Shakespeares, the philosophers and the scoffers, as well as the Papists, were extinguished by the Puritans. The theater gave way to the pulpit."

Having said all that, critics have neglected one important truth about the Puritans; they were not so much antagonistic to the theater *per se,* but to its gross misuse and abuse. Their objection was to the profanity and immorality displayed on the stage.

For quite some time, the Puritans were quite moderate on the subject of plays and dramas. Some of the Puritans themselves, like John Bale, one of the early Puritans that became an émigré on the continent, wrote plays like *Three Laws of Nature, Moses, and Christ,* which was a caustic attack on papal abuses. Even John Calvin allowed the production of a biblical play in Geneva. Marshall Knappen in his book *Tudor Puritanism* tells us that "the Puritan Inns of Court regularly produced plays and masques, as did their Oxford and Cambridge colleges."

The Puritans knew, like all others, that at best a stage drama could be a school of morals. It had often been in times past. Preachers would quote from a drama, as Paul quoted to his audience in Athens from the work of one of their own poets; and again, when writing to the Corinthians, he quoted from another Greek poet (1 Corinthians 15:33). The Puritans also knew that sometimes in the Old Testament the prophets taught by actions, and in the New Testament Jesus often spoke by parables. James Rees tells us in his book that the "story of the Prodigal Son is one of those beautifully told parables with which the Scriptures abound; it places before us, in a grand picture, scenes as sublime as they are impressive. It is a drama told."

In his day, Addison wrote in the *Spectator:* "Were our English stage but half so virtuous as that of the Greeks or Romans, we should quickly see the influence of it in the behavior of the politer part of mankind." And more than one author has stated that "the stage illustrates Scripture better than the pulpit."

The Puritans would also have known what Martin Luther had said on the subject of the stage. In his *Tishgesprable* he states: "In ancient times the dramatic art has been honoured by being made subservient to religion and morality, and in the most enlightened country of antiquity, Greece, the theaters were supported by the state."

And anyone distressed by certain actions and speeches witnessed on the stage, would find another statement by Luther to be helpful. He tells us in another book:

> ... indeed Christians ought not altogether to fly and abstain from comedies, because now and then gross tricks, and dallying passages are acted therein, for then it will follow that, by reason thereof, we should also abstain from reading the Bible.

What the Puritans condemned about the stage, as already stated, was the lifestyle of the actors, plus the nature of some of the plays themselves. Even one of the playwrights, Stephen Gosson, wrote a book on the subject, *School of Abuse,* in which he too condemned the nature of some of the plays. And Stubbs, who wrote the famous book *Anatomy of Abuses* calling the theaters "Satan's Synagogues," put in the preface of the first edition that "some kinds of plays, tragedies, and interludes" were "honest and very commendable." It was the extreme things seen on the stage, like wantonness, profanity, drunkenness, and men dressing as women in defiance of Mosaic Law, that kindled the ire of the Puritans.

There is one other fact that should be stated —

the fact that many of the other playwrights in London were not too happy with Shakespeare. This other group seemed to have dominated the drama world at the time, and were referred to as *The University Wits*. They were men who had all been either to Oxford or Cambridge University, like Christopher Marlowe, John Lyly, Thomas Nashe, Robert Greene, and others. They had the tendency to look down upon, and even disparage, any playwright or actor who had no university training. Shakespeare happened to be one of those, and Robert Greene made clear his own resentment toward him. In a posthumously published book, he gave a warning to three fellow "gentlemen" playwrights, one of them being Shakespeare:

> . . . trust them [the players] not; for there is an upstart crow, beautified with our feathers, that with his *Tiger's heart wrapt in a player's hide,* supposes he is as well able to bombast out a blank verse as the best of you: and being an absolute *Johannes Factotum,* is in his own conceit the only Shake-scene in a country.

Later, Henry Chettle, Greene's literary executor, "printed an apology for this slur on Shakespeare, with its pun on his name and its parody of a line from Henry IV, Part III." When Chettle later met Shakespeare in person, he found that Shakespeare's "demeanor no less civil than he, excellent in the quality he professes . . . divers of worship have reported his uprightness of dealing, which argues his honesty, and his facetious grace in writing . . ." (Joseph Rosenblum, *A Reader's Guide to Shakespeare,* pp.6–7).

It is important at this juncture to return with Shakespeare to Stratford, and to meet some of the men who shared his Anglican-Puritan views.

Shakespeare became a member of Holy Trinity Church, and later its lay-rector. He soon developed a very close acquaintance with its minister, Richard Byfield, and his family. Shakespeare soon realized, if he hadn't done so previously, that Richard Byfield and his two sons, Nicholas and Adoniram, were Puritans in their doctrine. At that time many Anglican clergy, including some of their bishops, had a close relationship and agreement with some of the Puritan leaders. It was not a full agreement on every issue, but a sort of general agreement, in particular regarding the relation of state and church. They seemed to agree with Calvin's position that the church authorities should be "amicably sharing the sovereignty with the wielders of the temporal sword." They also agreed that some of the Roman practices should be abolished, and certain doctrines like transubstantiation and clerical celibacy be rejected.

What helped, perhaps more than anything, to bring some of the Anglicans and Puritans together, was the religious storm that erupted during the reign of Queen Mary. Being a strong Roman Catholic, she did much to stamp out any Protestant doctrines that she considered heretical. Soon, some Protestants were imprisoned, and others burned at the stake. Often, Anglican clergy and Puritan preachers found themselves sharing the same prison. When the Act of Uniformity was passed in 1662, two thousand ministers seceded from their churches, including a number of Anglican divines. It will be of interest to many, that in that list were the two grandfathers of John Wesley.

The city of Stratford was located in Warwick-shire. If Essex was the headquarters of Puritanism, Warwickshire was certainly the hub. Many prominent political figures came from this area, including the Earl of Warwick, the Earl of Leicester, Robert Wigston of Woolston, John Hales of Coventry, and Job Throgmorton. Warwickshire was also the home of some well-known Puritan divines. There was Edward Lord and Hugh Clark, vicars of Woolston; John Hooke and Ephraim Hewet, vicars of Wroxhall; and, of course, Richard Byfield, vicar of Stratford. Not too far away was Oxford University, with Peter Martyr; and just a little further was Cambridge University, with scholars like Martin Bucer. These men were in close contact with the Reformers of Geneva — Bullinger, Calvin, and Beza.

And, of course, in the city of Warwick itself was one of the spiritual leaders of the whole Puritan movement, Thomas Cartwright. It was said that "there was not a nobleman or gentleman of quality in all the country that looked heavenward, or was of any account for religious learning but sought the company of Cartwright." Theodore Beza, Calvin's successor in Geneva, said of him: "I think the sun does not see a more learned man." In 1659 Cartwright had been made Lady Margaret Professor of Divinity in Cambridge University, but some of his strong Puritan beliefs disturbed a few of the authorities, and they protested to William Cecil, the Lord Chancellor of England. However, the reforming tide was so strong in Cambridge that thirty-three members of the university signed their names in support of Cartwright. He was allowed to continue, but it was not long afterward that they were able to remove him from office. Soon he had to go into exile, and was in Holland for eleven years, plus he spent some time in prison. It was after this that he moved to Warwick to live, and for years drew large congregations wherever he preached. As Wertenbaker tells us, Thomas Cartwright continued to believe that the Established Church of England was still the Church of God, and in spite of the dissolute lives of some of its members, he was against any kind of separation. His beliefs and doctrines, however, were strongly Puritan, and he was constantly ill-at-ease that the Established Church was governed by the throne through its archbishops and bishops. He believed that the local congregation should have a greater voice in selecting its own pastor, in enforcing church discipline, etc. It is of interest to note that when Thomas Carter published his book *Shakespeare, Puritan and Recusant,* he dedicated it to the Countess of Warwick, stating that her "ancestors rendered many and eminent services to the Puritan cause."

It was not thus uncommon in early seventeenth century England to find Anglican clergymen, from curates to bishops, adopting Puritan doctrines and principles. One noted Puritan minister was **Richard Baxter** of Kidderminster. He has often been referred to as *Mr. Puritan himself.* Most scholars agree that he was the outstanding Puritan of that period, a great preacher, and the most prolific author of the seventeenth century. He wrote one hundred sixty-eight books in all, with his *Christian Directory* being a million–word epic. Two of his books became classics.

Richard Baxter had been ordained into the ministry by the Bishop of Worcester, and served as a model pastor in Kidderminster for many years. At one point in his career he was offered the Bishopric of Hereford but declined it. As a matter of fact, he did not fully identify with the Episcopalians, nor with the Presbyterians, nor with the Independents.

Another noted Puritan was **James Ussher.** He was the Archbishop of Armagh, and the Primate of the Anglican Church of Ireland. He was noted for his godliness, his preeminent scholarship, and his strong Calvinistic theology. He was, for a long time, associated with a network of Puritan clergy, and was invited to become a member of the Westminster Assembly of Divines when they drew up the Westminster Confession of Faith. He did not attend, however, but had a great influence on it. As a matter of fact, according to William Barker, Ussher's "Irish Articles" "served as a model for much of the Westminster Confession of Faith."

In all, one hundred and twenty-one divines were appointed to the Westminster Assembly, with a number of them being Episcopalians, including a few Episcopalian bishops.

Another noted Puritan pastor and author was the Vicar of Lavenham, **William Gurnall.** He spent his whole ministerial life of thirty-five years in that one church. He became eminent as the author of one book, *The Christian in Complete Armour,* a book of over six hundred pages based on half of one chapter in Paul's Letter to the Ephesians. His classic is still being sold in Christian bookstores throughout the English-speaking world.

John Newton claimed that if he might read just

one book besides the Bible, he would choose *The Christian in Complete Armour.* J. C. Ryle, the Anglican Bishop of Liverpool, stated: "You really marvel how so much thought could be put into so few words." And the great Baptist preacher, Charles Haddon Spurgeon, wrote about the great Anglican-Puritan Gurnall that

> his work is peerless and priceless; every line is full of wisdom, every sentence is suggestive . . . the best thought-breeder in all our library. . . . I have often resorted to it when my own fire has been burning low, and I have seldom failed to find a glowing coal upon Gurnall's hearth.

Later, when two thousand pastors seceded from their churches, Gurnall was not among them. He became a lonely, solitary figure in that season of strife and controversy. In the ranks of the two thousand who seceded were prominent, theological giants, many of them close friends of William Gurnall. One can well imagine what followed — his Puritan friends had all left, and the Puritan Gurnall was left behind! His friends in both camps, Puritan and Anglican, began to suspect him. The Puritans considered him a traitor, the Anglicans a spy!

Such were the religious conflicts in Shakespeare's time. Pastors were often Puritan in their doctrine but Anglican/Episcopalian in their practice.

What about Shakespeare's own pastor, Richard Byfield of Stratford? Shakespeare was now retired from the stage and living in a new house in Stratford, called New Place. We learn that he was very close to his pastor and to his church. When the pastor was away, it was Shakespeare who gave a temporary home to the guest preachers. Most of those preachers, like Byfield and his two sons, were staunch Puritans in their doctrines. History reveals that Byfield's two sons were even more staunch than their father.

Nicholas Byfield became a prominent Puritan divine and commentator, and Adoniram Byfield even more so. He became a member of the London clergy, and was chosen chaplain to one of the regiments of the Parliamentary army, and was frequently referred to as the "fighting chaplain."

Later Adoniram Byfield was appointed scribe to the Assembly of Divines at Westminster, this being the Assembly that drew up the famous *Westminster Confession of Faith.* Many have declared this Confession to contain the purest distillation of Reformed doctrine available. Robert Shaw, in his book *The Reformed Faith,* praises its fidelity to Scripture, and states that "for logical fearlessness and power, for theological comprehension, and intellectual grandeur . . . it is second to none."

This **Confession** puts great emphasis on *liberty of conscience,* which was also one of the major Puritan principles. It states that human conscience was subject to the authority of God alone, and thus free from all subjection to the commands and traditions of men that were contrary to the Word of God. Such commands whether given by pope, priest, pastor, or king, judge, magistrate, even husband or parent, should not be tolerated. Civil and ecclesiastical authorities were no exception. At the same time the Confession stated that such authorities were necessary and even essential, and had certain prerogatives to perform, but all, without exception were subordinate to the sovereignty and laws of God.

When the Westminster Confession of Faith was presented to the House of Commons in London, it was Adoniram Byfield that was appointed by Parliament to deliver a copy to each member of the House, together with Scripture proofs.

Not all people treated Puritan divines with such respect. It is reported that on one occasion, Adoniram Byfield was stigmatized by Butler in his *Hudibras.* He was referred to as a very active zealot in the boisterous reign of Charles I, and that they published a portrait of him "with a wind mill on his head, and the devil blowing the sails."

There was another close relative of the family, also called Richard Byfield, who was "eminently distinguished as a zealous reformer, and a strenuous opposer of superstitious devices." For refusing to read the *Book of Sports,* he was suspended from his pastorate for "four years and four weeks." Later, however, Richard Byfield was chosen to be one of the members of that "brilliant constellation," the Westminster Assembly of Divines. Still later, he was appointed assistant to the commissioners of Surrey, with the task of ejecting scandalous ministers and schoolmasters.

There was one other interesting episode that happened in the career of Richard Byfield, and which underlines his Puritan convictions.

There was dissent between Richard Byfield and his patron, Sir John Evelyn, concerning a certain church matter. In the end, Byfield made a complaint to Oliver Cromwell, at that time the Lord Protector of England. As a result, Cromwell asked them both

*William
Shakespeare
and
His Bible*

to meet with him with the hope of reconciling their differences. Sir John's complaint was that Mr. Byfield had "reflected upon him in his sermons." Mr. Byfield declared solemnly that he had never had such intention in mind. Cromwell turned to Sir John, and said: "Sir, I doubt there is something indeed amiss; the word is penetrating and finds you out: search your ways."

It is told that when Cromwell finished his remarks, Sir John and Mr. Byfield, and all the others present, were reduced to tears. Cromwell made sure that they became good friends before he dismissed them, and then ordered his secretary to pay Sir John one hundred pounds towards the repair of the church.

Shakespeare's Knowledge and Choice of Bibles

4 For those who have read and studied Shakespeare's works, it is evident that he had accumulated vast knowledge on a number of subjects. We know that he must have been well informed on subjects like the military, politics, history, geography . . . and especially on legal and medical matters.

Back in 1858, William L. Rushton wrote a book entitled *Shakespeare a Lawyer,* stating that Shakespeare must have had technical knowledge of the law, covering various fields like property law, statute law, criminal law, and common law. A year later, in 1859, a legal scholar, John Lord Campbell, wrote a book of one hundred forty-six pages, entitled *Shakespeare's Legal Acquirements Considered.*

In the year 1865, medical doctor Charles W. Stearns authored a book with the title *Shakespeare's Medical Knowledge.*

More scholars, however, have written on Shakespeare's knowledge of religion, and in particular his knowledge of the Holy Bible.

Over a century ago, Bishop Wordsworth issued a statement that was summarized later in a book by F. J. Furnivall, stating:

> No book is so often quoted or alluded to by Shakespeare as the Bible. Not only does he mention Holy Writ four times, Scripture three times, the Word three times, the Book of Life once, the Book nine times, "It is Written" once; not only does he quote Bible passages in his plays . . . but he accepts, or makes his characters accept, the whole scheme of salvation set forth in the Jewish and Christian Testaments, and the stories of the Apocrypha too.

James Buchan Brown, writing over a hundred years ago, stated:

> So perfectly impregnated with the leaven of the Bible are his works, that we can scarcely open them, as if by accident, without encountering one or other of its great truths, which his genius has assimilated and reproduced in words that seem to renew its authority and strengthen its claims upon men's attention.

Another author testified that Shakespeare's knowledge of the Bible was so complete that he would know a word if it only existed once in all the sixty-six books! He went on to give an example: the word *bravery* is only found once in Scripture, and that in Isaiah 3:18. But Shakespeare knew it, and it is found in his play, *The Taming of the Shrew*, Act IV Scene 3.

In 1876, James Rees wrote a book, *Shakespeare and the Bible,* and tells us:

Shakespeare has given us a vast amount of intellectual wealth — he is quoted at the bar, the rostrum, and the pulpit . . . but many of his bright and beautiful gems have shone for ages in different forms in that sacred volume . . . the Scriptures of the Old and New Testament beneath his hand the gems of old were set anew.

Later, in 1897, Thomas Carter could write in his book *Shakespeare, Puritan and Recusant* that "no writer has assimilated the thoughts and reproduced the words of Holy Scripture *more copiously than Shakespeare.*"

And a hundred years later, at the end of the twentieth century, no less a scholar than Dr. Naseeb Shaheen, professor of English at the University of Memphis, Tennessee, states regarding Shakespeare:

Not only is the range of his biblical references impressive, but also the aptness with which he makes them. Hamlet and Othello have more than fifty biblical references. No study of Shakespeare's plays is complete that ignores Shakespeare's use of Scripture.

Perhaps the most radiant statement of all was that by an unknown author, who said that just as the prophets and the apostles were inspired of God to compose their work to the Book of Books, so was Shakespeare inspired by the Book of Books to compose the second best book in the English language! He called it "a secular Bible."

It has been claimed that of the sixty-six books of the Bible, Shakespeare quoted from fifty-seven of them. Scholars, by studying his plays, have found in them a total of twelve hundred biblical references. And, of course, Shakespeare's Bible included the *Apocrypha* as well, with quotations from 2 Esdras, Tobit, Judith, Wisdom, 1 and 2 Maccabees, and extensively from Ecclesiasticus.

Perhaps surpassing the comments made by the scholars of the last four centuries are the words of the Almighty God Himself, as quoted by His ancient prophet, Isaiah (57:19): **"I create the fruit of the lips."**

❖ ❖ ❖ ❖ ❖

From his plays, we also know that Shakespeare was not only acquainted with the Bible, including its Apocrypha, but also with books like *Foxe's Book of Martyrs*.

When Shakespeare wrote his play *King John*, it was the current belief in England that King John, because of his opposition to the papacy, had been poisoned by a monk. In the play, Hubert, a citizen of Angers, tells Philip the Bastard:

> *A monk, I tell you, a resolved villain,*
> *Whose bowels suddenly burst out: the king*
> *Yet speaks and peradventure may recover.*

Although it was the popular belief that the king had been poisoned, Dr. Shaheen and others are convinced that Shakespeare took the view of the Puritan John Foxe that it was the monk who was poisoned, and whose bowels burst.

And, of course, Shakespeare was also aware, from his knowledge of the Bible, of how Judas Iscariot died, as recorded in Acts 1:18.

Knowing that Shakespeare was so unusually knowledgeable in the Bible, it is appropriate to ask which version of the Bible he used? In the days of Shakespeare, there were a few versions available in the English language.

The first to appear was the **Wycliffe Bible.** This was translated in 1384, but was not actually printed until 1731. Wycliffe translated it from the Latin Vulgate, and, of course, it was handwritten. Copies took ten months to make. Wycliffe thus shares with Chaucer the glory of creative service in English literature. It has been said that if Chaucer was the father of English poetry, Wycliffe was the father of English prose.

Very soon after its appearance, Wycliffe's Bible was prohibited by law in England. In 1408 the Provisional Council at Oxford prohibited an English translation of the Bible on pain of excommunication and a trial for heresy. Archbishop Arundel was particularly critical, and referred to Wycliffe's work as that of *anti-Christ.* He called Wycliffe "that wretched and pestilent fellow of damnable memory, son of the old serpent, and the very herald and child of anti-Christ . . . who crowned his wickedness by translating the Scriptures into the mother tongue." Wycliffe must have made quite an impact to merit such a choice eulogy! Shakespeare was probably aware of the existence of the Wycliffe Bible, in its handwritten form, but it is doubtful if he ever quoted from it.

The next to appear was the **Tyndale Bible** in 1526. This was translated directly from the Hebrew and the Greek. Tyndale was also the first to produce a *printed English Bible*. It was not done in England, however, but on the continent of Europe. In spite of this, hundreds of copies were smuggled into England, often hidden in bales of merchandise. The Tyndale version was written in matchless style and had a profound influence on the development of the English language.

Unfortunately, William Tyndale was strangled to death, and then buried as a martyr, before he was able to complete the whole Bible. His last words were: *"Lord, open the King of England's eyes."* When a celebrated clergyman was sent to convert Tyndale, he was told: *"If God spares my life, I will take care that a ploughboy shall know more of the Scriptures than you do."*

Nine years later followed the **Coverdale Bible,** which was written in 1535 and licensed in 1537. This was translated from the German and from the Latin Vulgate. It was the first English Bible to introduce chapter summaries. Coverdale also separated the Apocrypha from the Old Testament, and placed it between the Old and the New Testaments. The Bible was dedicated to King Henry VIII, but it was not as vigorous a translation as the Tyndale Bible.

Two years later, in 1537, followed the **Matthew Bible.** Thomas Matthew was a pseudonym taken by the editor, John Rogers. It was a sort of combination of the Tyndale and Coverdale versions. At the request of Archbishop Cranmer it was granted the royal license. It was thus the first *English Authorized Version.* Many of its notes, however, were bitterly opposed, and later John Rogers was destined to become the first martyr during the reign of Queen Mary.

Two years later, in 1539, the **Great Bible** appeared. It is believed it was done on the orders of Thomas Cromwell and Archbishop Cranmer. Taking part in its translation and production was Miles Coverdale, revising the Matthew Bible *but without its notes*. It was primarily based, however, on the Tyndale Bible, and a year later, in 1540, it became the official Bible of the English Church. It was called the Great Bible because of its size. Thomas Cromwell instructed the clergy to provide a copy for every church in the land, so that the parishioners could read it. King Henry VIII ordered each copy to be chained to the reading desk of every church. For this purpose, eleven thousand copies were required. For the second edition, and all five subsequent editions, an impressive preface was written by Archbishop Cranmer, and often the Great Bible would then be referred to as the Cranmer Bible.

In 1568 the **Bishop's Bible** appeared, translated by a number of prominent and scholarly bishops of the Established Church of England. This was under the superintendence of Archbishop Parker. It was large in size and very costly. It is said that it had a life of some forty years and passed through nineteen editions. Although translated by some scholarly men, it did not satisfy most scholars, and the general public felt it was ill-suited for them.

❖ ❖ ❖ ❖ ❖

It is possible that Shakespeare knew *something* about all these Bibles and could well have consulted a *few* of them. As stated, it is highly doubtful if he had ever seen the Wycliffe Bible, and there is no evidence that he ever quoted from it. The **King James**

Version, which was the authorized version of the Church of England, did not appear until 1611, just five years before Shakespeare's death. By that time most of his literary work had already been completed and he was in retirement in Stratford. The same could be said of the Roman Catholic **Douai Bible,** which was published in France about a year before the King James Version in England.

The very few who still persist in the belief that Shakespeare belonged to the Old Faith remind us that the **Rheims New Testament** had already been translated into English in 1582, and was thus available to him. Just as Protestants exiled by Queen Mary went to the continent and produced their Geneva Version, so the Roman Catholics exiled by Queen Elizabeth I sought to bring out a vernacular translation of their own. Of the many schools and seminaries founded on the continent by the Roman Catholic exiles, the most important was the one at Douai, in northern France. Permission was obtained from the pope to undertake the English translation of the Bible, and in 1582 the New Testament was published in Rheims, where the college was located from 1578 to 1593.

This new version was based on the Latin Vulgate, and not on the original Hebrew and Greek. Although scholarly, many felt it was pedantic and empesé, and according to Dr. Shaheen, "many passages were altogether unintelligible." Some of the words contained in it could only be understood by people proficient in Latin. Other words used were highly extravagant. As an example, the Lord's Prayer included this sentence: "Give us to day our supersubstantial bread."

As a matter of fact, Dr. Shaheen doubts very much whether Shakespeare was even acquainted with the Rheims Bible. He states in his book *Biblical References in Shakespeare's History Plays* (published by University of Delaware Press, 1989):

> Whenever a biblical reference in Shakespeare appears to be closest to both the Rheims and the Geneva versions of the day, it is not because Shakespeare possessed a copy of the Rheims as a few scholars claim, but because the translators of the Rheims frequently borrowed Geneva readings in their translation, although at the same time they attacked all Protestant translations.

It must also be remembered that whereas the Geneva Bible was dedicated to Queen Elizabeth I, possession of a Rheims New Testament was suspect during her reign. Priests found with copies of it were imprisoned.

❖ ❖ ❖ ❖ ❖

This brings us now to the **Geneva Version,** known to most in England in those days as the **Puritan Bible.**

It first appeared in 1560, and soon became the most popular and scholarly translation of the English Bible. It was the one used in most of the homes of England, and also used and quoted from by the most prominent literary figures of the Elizabethan period. Even when the Bishop's Bible came out a few years later and became the official Bible of the Established Church of England, the Puritan Bible was still considered superior, with the Bishop's Bible second best!

Queen Mary came to power in 1553, and very soon there was prohibition against the use of English Bibles. As a result, men like John Rogers, Thomas Cranmer, and others were executed. Queen Mary was a strict and devout Roman Catholic, and during her reign close to a thousand Englishmen had to flee to the continent for refuge. Some went to Germany, and some to Switzerland. John Foxe fled to Basle in Switzerland, and there wrote his masterpiece, *The Book of Martyrs.* Others like John Knox, William Whittingham, Anthony Gilby, Christopher Goodman, Thomas Cole, and Miles Coverdale made their way to Geneva. John Knox became pastor of the English Church in Geneva, with two hundred and thirty-three exiles as members.

Under John Calvin, Geneva became a hive of activity for Bible translators. The Bible was soon translated into Italian, Spanish, French . . . at least twenty-two editions of the French Bible were made during the 1550s.

The English translation appeared in 1560, after constant work, day and night, for two years. One of those most actively interested in it was John Bodley, the father of the founder of the Bodleian Library in Oxford.

The English Bible was named the Geneva Bible, or sometimes the Geneva Version. It was dedicated to Queen Elizabeth I, although oddly enough it was her predecessor, "Bloody Mary," who was indirectly responsible — she was the one who sent the exiles to Geneva in the first place!

A further word should be said about the translators. They do not identify themselves, but they are believed to be the ones already mentioned as exiles, with William Whittingham, a brother-in-law to John Calvin, as the general editor. They used the work of many scholars, with Whittingham and Gilby among the most competent linguists of the day. Later, a large number of the King James Bible renderings followed the Geneva Version.

The style was clear, crisp, and vigorous. It was not studded in any way with foreign terms, but written in the tome of the mother tongue. It has been said that its power lay in its simplicity, and its grandeur in its familiar idioms.

The Geneva Bible had many distinctives that contributed to its popularity:

- ❖ It was a scholarly translation, direct from the Hebrew and Greek.
- ❖ Instead of being a large, unwieldy folio volume, it was a handy quarto.
- ❖ It was the first English Bible printed in Roman type.
- ❖ It was the first English Bible divided into chapters and verses.
- ❖ It supplied *words* to complete the sense in English; these were inserted in *italics*.
- ❖ It had arguments preceding each book and each chapter.
- ❖ It had notable words on the top of each page.
- ❖ It contained a commentary and concordance . . . and Sternhold and Hopkins' Metrical Psalms with music.
- ❖ It contained a chronology of the years, twenty-six woodcuts, and five maps.
- ❖ It had scriptural aids in the margin, plus three hundred thousand words of marginal

notes. These notes were changed from time to time, like those that identified the *Beast* of the Book of Revelation with a particular pope, e.g. Pope Boniface VIII.

Many, if not most, of the marginal notes had been copied from Calvin's French Bible. They supplied the Puritans with extra ammunition for their future attacks on the papacy and the episcopacy. One example referred to by Knappen, is the Geneva Version notes on the *locusts of the Book of Revelation.* According to marginal notes, the locusts did not refer only to heretics, but also to "Archbishops, and Bishops, Doctors, Bachelors, and Masters which forsake Christ to maintain false doctrine."

When King James held a conference at Hampton Court (1604) giving orders for an Authorized Version of the English Bible, he made it clear that there were to be no *marginal notes.* He referred to some of the notes in the Geneva Bible as being partial, untrue, seditious, and savoring too much of dangerous and traitorous conceits. He gave them two examples:

⬥ Exodus 1:19 — The Geneva marginal note allowed disobedience to kings.

⬥ 2 Chronicles 15:16 — The Geneva Bible censured King Asa for merely *deposing* his mother, when he should have executed her. King James may well have remembered what happened to his own mother, Mary Queen of Scots.

Regarding the king's remarks, there was criticism from some of the Puritans present at the conference, who had expected greater cooperation from King James, knowing that he had been educated in Scotland under Presbyterian divines. When they suggested to him that they should call a general church assembly, he emphatically refused. He told them, "If you aim at a Scottish Presbytery, it agreeth as well with monarchy as God with the devil."

In spite of some criticism from the Anglican Church, *Bishop Westcott* expressed the opinion of most when he gave his own judgment of the Geneva Bible: *"Pure and vigorous in style, and, if slightly tinged with Calvinistic doctrine, yet on the whole neither unjust nor illiberal."*

As already stated, the Geneva Bible became very popular with the people — as a matter of fact, the most popular in England. Between 1560 and the Civil War, one hundred and sixty editions were published. If the Bishop's Bible was the one used in the churches of England, it was the Puritan Bible that was used in the homes of England.

Perhaps one more fact should be added here. In 1576 Laurence Tomson published a revised version of the Geneva New Testament. Dr. Shaheen is one of the few current scholars who has studied this version with great diligence, and came to the conclusion that its importance was not in the text but in the notes that accompanied the text. He believes that the only distinguishing feature of the text was that Tomson followed Beza (Calvin's successor) in emphasizing the Greek definitive article. But for this characteristic, Tomson's New Testament is much like the Geneva New Testament. A short time after publishing his version, Tomson's New Testament was bound with the Geneva Old Testament and

William
Shakespeare
and
His Bible

Apocrypha and became known as the Geneva-Tomson Bible.

We shall prove later that Shakespeare used the Geneva Bible, but it is fairly accurate to say that he had consulted the Tomson New Testament as well, since a number of his plays resemble the information found in *Tomson's notes*.

Shakespeare and
the Puritan Bible

5No one can doubt that the influence of the
Geneva Bible, or the Geneva Version as it
was often called, was irrefutable. It had a
big influence on the King James Version.
Butterworth stated that the books of the prophets
in the Geneva Bible were superior to that in the King
James Bible. He went on to give the statistics of the
material incorporated into the King James Bible, and
came up with the following result.

Wycliffe Bible	4%
Coverdale Bible	13%
Tyndale Bible	18%
Geneva Bible	19%

This makes a total of sixty-one percent, allowing only
thirty-nine percent for *new material* in the King
James Bible.

Needless to say, the Geneva Version had a great
influence and impact on the preachers and commentators of England at that time. The vast majority
preferred reading and quoting from the Geneva than
from any other version available.

It had an influence also on the soldiers in the Parliamentary army during the Protectorate of Oliver Cromwell. Each soldier carried a copy of the *Soldier's Pocket Bible* issued in 1643. This consisted of a selection of extracts from the Geneva Bible.

As previously stated, it had an influence on much of the literature of the sixteenth and seventeenth centuries. It was invariably the Geneva Bible that was used by Edmund Spenser, John Bunyan, John Milton, and others. It should be added that Milton was influenced not only by the Geneva text, but by the marginal notes as well. This was particularly evident in *Paradise Lost* and *Samson Agonistes*.

The influence of the Geneva Bible was not only felt in England, but in Wales and Ireland also, and particularly in Scotland. The Geneva was the version actually chosen as the one to be read in the churches of Scotland. An act of Parliament made it mandatory in Scotland that "every householder worth three hundred marks of yearly rent, every yeoman and burger worth five hundred stock should have in his home a Bible and Psalm Book in the vernacular tongue, under a penalty of ten pounds."

Its influence very soon spread to America as well. The Geneva was the favored Bible of both the *Plymouth* and the *Virginia* settlements. It was the Bible used on board the *Mayflower,* and it was with their hands on that Bible that they endorsed the **Mayflower Compact.**

❖ ❖ ❖ ❖ ❖

The question of interest to us now is to ask: **Which version did Shakespeare use?**

He could well have known, of course, the Tyndale Bible, the Great Bible and the Bishop's Bible. It seems he did use a little of the Bishop's Bible in his earlier plays. It is highly doubtful, as we have already seen, that he used the Douai Bible or the King James Bible at all, both of which appeared late in his life.

Scholars are of the opinion that whereas Shakespeare may have known some of the other versions, it was the **Puritan Bible,** namely the **Geneva Version** that he normally used. Much has been written on this, but for the sake of brevity, we will confine our remarks to two authors, one from the nineteenth century and one from the twentieth.

In the late nineteenth century, Thomas Carter, in his book *Shakespeare and Holy Scripture,* stated that "no writer has assimilated the thoughts and reproduced the words of Holy Scripture more copiously than Shakespeare." He then adds: "I have studied every line in the plays in order to trace out how far this indebtedness extends and, after a careful comparison, have come to the conclusion that *the Geneva Bible was the version used by Shakespeare.*"

After an extensive study of Shakespeare's plays in the late twentieth century, Dr. Naseeb Shaheen, professor of English at Memphis State University, has come to the same conclusion that Shakespeare *"referred to the Geneva Bible more often than any other version."* Many other authors have come to the identical conclusion.

We shall now quote from a few of Shakespeare's plays to demonstrate how indebted he was to the Geneva Bible. By so doing, we may also learn something about the religious character of Shakespeare himself. It has been well said that a man's character can be assumed "from the monuments he left behind." Shakespeare left a large number of such monuments, particularly the plays he authored.

Examples:

In Shakespeare's play *King Henry VI*, Part 1, the Duke of Alençon tells Charles (later king of France): *"All France will be replete with mirth and joy when they shall hear how we have **play'd the men.**"*

Shakespeare undoubtedly recalled a verse he knew in the Old Testament. In 1 Samuel 4:9 he recalled the words: "Be strong and *play the men.*" He had to have been using the Geneva Bible since no other version available at the time had that phrase. All the other versions had either, "Be strong now *and manly*" or *"Quit yourselves like men,"* which is the King James Version also.

❖ ❖ ❖ ❖ ❖

In *Richard II*, the Duchess of Gloucester says to John of Gaunt: *". . . and his summer **leaves all faded."***

In all probability Shakespeare had in mind the words in Psalm 1:3. In his Geneva Version he would read: ". . . whose *leafe shall not fade."* All the other Bible Versions extant at that time, read, "Whose leaves are *fallen awaye."* When the King James Version appeared, it read, "his leaf shall *not wither."*

❖ ❖ ❖ ❖ ❖

Also in the play *Richard II,* King Richard tells Thomas Mowbray, the Duke of Norfolk: *"Rage must be withstood: Give me his gage; lions make **leopards** tame."*

Mowbray answers him: *"Yea, but not change his spots."*

Shakespeare must have remembered the verse in Jeremiah 13:23, where the Geneva was the only version to use the word *leopard*. All the previous versions used the word *cat o' the mountain*.

❖ ❖ ❖ ❖ ❖

In *King Henry IV*, Henry the Prince of Wales tells Sir John Falstaff: *"I see a good **amendment** of life in thee."*

Again, all versions prior to the Geneva, and even King James Version afterwards, use the term *repent*. Examples would be Matthew 3:8,11; Acts 3:19, 26:20, etc. The Geneva Bible reads: "Amend your lives therefore. . . ."

❖ ❖ ❖ ❖ ❖

In the same play, *King Henry IV*, Sir John Falstaff tells Bardolph:

> *You would think that I had a hundred and fifty tattered prodigals lately come from swine-keeping, from eating draff and **husks**.*

Clearly Shakespeare knew the famous parable of Jesus regarding the prodigal son found in Luke 15. He had to be quoting from the Geneva Version, since it was the first English version to use the word *huskes*. All the other versions, Coverdale, Matthew, Cranmer, the Bishop's, and the Great Bible used the word *cods*. Later, Rheims and the KJV followed the Geneva Bible.

In *The Merchant of Venice,* Shylock speaks to Bassanio and refers to: *". . . your prophet **the Nazarite.**"* This too is an obvious quotation from the Geneva Bible, since all the other versions (including the KJV) refer to the prophet as the *Nazarene* not *Nazarite.*

Many have claimed that the use of the word *Nazarite* in reference to Jesus here was a mistake on the part of Shakespeare. They state that he should have used the term *Nazarene.* Bishop Wordsworth asks an interesting question: "Had our poet any reason for making use of the term Nazarite rather than Nazarene . . . or was it merely a mistake?"

Shakespeare, however, knew his Bible too well to make a mistake, and well enough to know that there was a distinction between the words Nazarene and Nazarite.

The word *Nazarene* is from the Greek, meaning he was from the town of *Nazareth.* It is used a number of times in the Gospel of Mark (10:47; 14:67; 16:6). The word *Nazarite,* on the other hand, referred not to the town of Nazareth but to a consecrated group of believers. In Judges 13:5, where it refers to Samson, we read: "For the child shall be *a Nazarite* unto God from the womb." In the Book of Numbers, chapter six, we are given more explicit details of what a vow of a Nazarite meant. He is consecrated to the Lord, and separated from many earthly things.

In the Geneva Bible there is a note in the margin, referring to the word *Nazarite* in Numbers 6:2, saying: *"which figure was accomplished in Christ."* And also a marginal note to Judges 13:5, where

Calvin says of a Nazarite: *"Christ is the original model."*

What is interesting about the New Testament use of the word is that in Matthew 2:23, the King James Version reads: *"He shall be called a Nazarene."* But all the early versions, Wycliffe, Tyndale, Cranmer, Geneva, and even Rheims has, *"He shall be called a Nazarite."*

In Acts 24:5, the Apostle Paul is accused by the high priest and the elders before Felix, the procurator of Judea. The KJV reads: "For we have found this man a pestilent fellow, and a mover of sedition among all the Jews throughout the world, and a ringleader of the *sect of the Nazarenes.*" This was also the word used by Wycliffe and Rheims. All the other versions, however, give the correct rendering: *"the Nazarites."*

In view of this, most scholars have to admit that it was no mistake on the part of Shakespeare. He was following the versions of his day. And of those versions, only the Geneva is consistent throughout.

Thomas Carter makes one other interesting point about Shylock using the word *Nazarite.* When Bassanio told him: "If it please you to dine with us," Shylock answers him:

Yes, to smell pork, to eat of the habitation which your prophet the Nazarite conjured the devil into. . . .

Shylock, says Carter,

. . . is not using the term *Nazarite* as a reproach, but for the purpose of showing that the highest

Christian example warranted him in abstaining from that intercourse which was forbidden to a consecrated race. He, as a Jew, felt as it were, the obligation of the Nazarite upon him, and he emphasizes the point by showing that the Christian Nazarite thought as he did.

Shylock's statement also reveals the connection between *pork* and the *devil,* no doubt alluding to the miracle of Christ casting out the *demons* from the man of Gadara, and sending them into the *swine,* and finally into the sea.

❖ ❖ ❖ ❖ ❖

In *Hamlet,* we find a word never used in our day, and rarely used in Shakespeare's day. Of all the versions of the Bible, it is only used in the Geneva.

In the play, Hamlet speaks, and begins with a very familiar phrase: "To be, or not to be, that is the question." Later in the speech, he says: *"Who would* **fardels** *bear, To grunt and sweat under a weary life"*

Sometimes the word would be spelled *fardels* and sometimes *fardles.* The probable scriptural reference would be in the Book of Acts, when the Apostle Paul set out on his last journey to Jerusalem. His friends feared that he would not return, and that they would never see his face again. In chapter twenty-one, verses fourteen and fifteen, we read in the Geneva Bible: "So when he would not be persuaded we ceased saying, The will of the Lord be done. And after those dayes we trussed up our *fardels* and went up to Hierusalem."

All the other versions vary on this one word:

Wycliffe — "we were made ready."
Tyndale — "we made ourselves ready."
Cranmer — "we took up our burthens."
Rheims — "being prepared."
KJV — "we took up our carriages."

In our day, the New King James Version reads: "And after those days *we packed* and went up to Jerusalem." And the New English Bible: *"we packed our baggage."* And the New International Version: "after this, we got ready and went up to Jerusalem."

❖ ❖ ❖ ❖ ❖

In *Othello* we have another example of Shakespeare's amazing knowledge of the Puritan Bible. Toward the end of the final act, Othello tells Lodovico, a nobleman of Venice, to speak of him just as he was. He admits that he had "loved not wisely, but too well." He also admits being "perplexed in the extreme," and: *"Like the base Indian, threw a pearl away richer than all his tribe . . ."*

That is how it read in the Quarto of 1622. Theobald proposed, however, the word *Judian* instead of the word *Indian*. Thomas Carter, in his book, believes that Theobald, by using the word *Judian*, was alluding to Herod, "who in a fit of blind jealousy, threw away such a jewel of a wife as Marianne was to him."

Carter himself, however, did not believe that. He doesn't believe that Othello was referring to Herod at all, since Herod was not a Judean. Herod might have been king of Judea, but he himself was actually an Idumean. The Pharisees often reproached the Herods as "half-Jews."

Those who still assert that *Indian* was the right word may have a problem with the word that precedes it — the word *base*. A pearl-fisher in India could possibly throw away a rich pearl foolishly, but he would hardly be considered *base* for doing so.

Many believe that Shakespeare was, in all probability, referring to the *"base Judean"* and that Judean would be Judas Iscariot. All the other disciples of Jesus came from Galilee. Judas' home was in Kerioth, located near the southern border of Judea. And, of course, no other character in history would have a better claim to the word *base* than Judas. It denotes vileness and infamy. When Judas betrayed his Master, he certainly *"threw a pearl away, richer than all his tribe."*

One could also add another fact: Othello, like Judas, committed suicide. Othello's final words before doing so were: *"I kiss'd thee, ere I kill'd thee."*

The same thing happened in the Garden of Gethsemane. We read of Judas in the Geneva Version of Matthew 26:49: ". . . forthwith he came to Jesus, and said, God save Thee, Master, and kissed Him."

❖ ❖ ❖ ❖ ❖

Leading directly from this, one finds in the play *MacBeth*, Rosse, a nobleman of Scotland, saying: *"God save the King!"*

If Shakespeare is here using the words found in Matthew 27:29, then he had to be using the Geneva Bible. It was the only one that stated: *"God save Thee King of the Jews."* All the other Bible Version, including the King James Version, state: *"Hail, King of the Jews."*

❖ ❖ ❖ ❖ ❖

Also in the play *MacBeth,* we read of Lady Macbeth walking in her sleep. When her gentlewoman was asked by her doctor, what, at any time, had she heard Lady Macbeth say, she answered:

> *That, Sir, which I will not report after her.*

> *DOCTOR: You may, to me; and 'tis most meet*
> *you should.*

> *GENTLEWOMAN: Neither to you, nor any one;*
> *having no witness to confirm my speech.*

It is fairly clear that Shakespeare here was using Matthew 18:16 as a reference where it reads in the King James Version: ". . . in the mouth of two or three witnesses every word *may be established.*" Tyndale and Cranmer also used the word *established.* Wycliffe and Rheims had *stand.* Geneva is the only version that uses the word *confirmed.*

❖ ❖ ❖ ❖ ❖

In the play *King Lear,* the king speaks to Edgar: *"Is man no more than this? Consider him well."*
    Shakespeare was undoubtedly quoting a verse from the Letter to the Hebrews (2:6). It reads in the King James Version: "What is man, that thou art mindful of him? or the son of man, *that thou visitest him?*"
    Most of the Bible versions use the same words as the King James Version: *visitest him.* Tyndale

used: *mindful of him.* It is only the Geneva Version that has the word used by Shakespeare: *consider him.*

It is interesting to add here, that in his latest book Harold Bloom, a professor at Yale University, states in his chapter on *King Lear* that the playwright Shakespeare here is in "debt to the laments of the aged King Solomon in the Geneva Bible. The connection between the two kings establishes what is often overlooked about Lear: his grandeur."

❖ ❖ ❖ ❖ ❖

In the play *King Henry IV,* Part 2, Lord Mowbray speaks to the Archbishop of York:

> *We shall be **winnow'd** with so rough a wind*
> *That even our corn shall seem as light as chaff*
> *And good from bad find no partition.*

Here is a reference, no doubt, to a verse in the Geneva Version, Luke 23:31: "And the Lord said, Simon, Simon, behold Satan hath desired you, to *winnow* you as wheat."

Again, the Geneva Version stands alone in this. The other versions — Tyndale, Cranmer, Rheims, and even the King James Version — use the words *"sift you,* as it were wheat."

❖ ❖ ❖ ❖ ❖

Of the other examples available from different plays, we'll close with one more. It is from *King Henry VI,* Part 1. Lord Talbot, who appears in the play as a man of both physical and moral excellence, and known as "the terror of the French," addresses some of the English leaders: *"God is our **fortress**, in whose conquering name let us resolve to scale their flinty bulwarks."*

If Shakespeare had 2 Samuel 22:2 in mind, "The Lord is my rock and my fortress," then he is definitely using the Puritan Bible, because all the other versions use the word *castle.* When the King James Version appeared in 1611, it followed the Geneva.

❖ ❖ ❖ ❖ ❖

As stated, there are many other words found in the plays of Shakespeare that prove beyond all possible doubt that most of his biblical vocabulary came from the Puritan Bible. In addition, he was equally acquainted with the marginal notes of the Puritan Bible.

Shakespeare and the Clergy

6 For those who believe that Shakespeare was a totally irreligious man, the main argument they submit is his constant at tack on the clergy, cardinals, bishops, priests, friars . . . in play after play. To claim that he was anti-Catholic would be far more credible than to claim that he was an atheist.

W. J. Birch claims in his book *An Inquiry into the Philosophy and Religion of Shakespeare* that Shakespeare considered members of the priesthood as not being suitable to their profession, that they were *more philosophers than priests.* And as for the Anglican clergy, he considered them *ridiculous.*

Early in the play *King Henry V,* we find the Archbishop of Canterbury telling his ecclesiastical friend, the Bishop of Ely, of the manifest change in Henry's character since becoming king. The bishop immediately tells him it is due to natural causes.

And so the Prince obscured his contemplation
Under the veil of wildness, which, no doubt,

Grew like the summer grass, fastest by night,
Unseen, yet crescive in his faculty.

The Archbishop responds: *"It must be so, for miracles are ceased."* No longer is it God at work, but natural causes! It is no wonder that the Anglican priesthood were ill-at-ease with some of Shakespeare's plays. Later examples will explain why the Roman Catholic priests were even more ill-at-ease. They no doubt suspected Shakespeare of being in the Puritan fold. They knew exactly what the Puritans thought of them, and now they heard the same accusations from Shakespeare. When they listened to his plays, they soon realized that Shakespeare was using the Puritan Bible, and that in itself was anathema to them.

It is true to say that what Shakespeare did actually criticize was the sordid side of the priesthood. There is no evidence anywhere that he was criticizing true religion. He probably would have agreed with Francis Bacon in one of his essays:

They that deny a God, destroy man's nobility;
for certainly man is of kin to the beasts by his
body: and, if he be not of kin to God by his spirit,
he is a base and ignoble creature.

Shakespeare's portrait of the clergy, Roman Catholic and Anglican, as not being suitable to their profession, is certainly akin to the portrait given by the Puritans. Nobody proclaimed more often than the Puritans that the clergymen of Rome and of the Established Church in England, were ill-informed in their knowledge of the Bible, and totally ineffective in their preaching. All too often they would read from

—83—

the Prayer Book rather than preach from the Bible.

In 1578 the county of Cornwall sent a petition to Parliament in London: "Therefore from far we come beseeching this honourable House to dispossess these dumb dogs and ravenous wolves, and appoint us faithful ministers who may peaceably preach the Word of God."

A year later, in 1579, the students in Cambridge University referred to unlearned ministers as "the scum of the people," and "were preferred to the learned and godly ones because they refused to submit to the subscriptions demanded by the ecclesiastical authorities."

Statements of that nature reminds us of Thersites telling Ajax in the play *Troilus and Cressida:* "I think thy horse will sooner con an oration than thou learn a prayer without book."

John Hooper made a survey of three hundred and eleven Anglican clergymen and found an appalling ignorance:

- ❖ 171 of them could not recite the Ten Commandments
- ❖ 33 of them had no idea where the Ten Commandments could be found
- ❖ 30 had no idea where the Lord's Prayer appeared in the Bible
- ❖ 10 could not recite the Lord's Prayer

Marcus Loane, who was the Primate of the Church of England in Australia, in his book *Makers of Puritan History,* reveals a lot about the Church of England clergy during the Puritan era. He states that the very church where Richard Baxter had been baptized "was served by four readers, . . . all were ignorant; two were immoral." The church where Baxter's father grew up had a reader "who was old and blind, who read the prayers by heart and did not preach at all."

Marcus Loane states that they had to get help from other readers "who came and went in a disgraceful succession." When Richard Baxter himself wrote on the same subject, he stated: "We changed them oft, because they were fonder of the tavern than of books or sermons."

What impressed Baxter more than anything was the time when the people scoffed at his father for being "a Puritan or a Precision." Baxter knew only too well that his father could read the Scripture better than his accusers.

During that same period, Puritan preachers were categorized as "godly and learned." Puritan concern was for a college-educated clergy. Six years after the Puritans landed in Massachusetts, they founded Harvard University, named after one of their own leaders, John Harvard. They dreaded an "illiterate ministry." William Ames expressed it this way: "The receiving of the Word consists of two parts: attention of mind and intention of will." In New England, Cotton Mather praised John Cotton because his sermons "all smelt of the lamp."

By intellectual preaching, the Puritans did not imply academic or theoretic preaching. What they meant was that a preacher's mind should be utterly submitted to the mighty influences of revealed truth. It meant that Puritan preaching had to be the product of an arduous, mental exercise. The Puritan preacher had to be concerned with truth, and he knew that truth demanded intellectual understanding and long hours of study. He knew that before he

could hope to preach the truth, he had first to understand the truth. Or as Edward Marbury expressed
it so succinctly: "A faithful minister must see before
he say."

Nothing angered the Puritans as much as unworthy clergy, trafficking in unworthy things, and
adulterating the oracles of God. They firmly believed
in a scriptural, prayerful, and energetic ministry.
John Owen, who was the vice-chancellor of Oxford
University, said: "He that is more frequent in his
pulpit to his people than he is in his closet for his
people is but a sorry watchman."

It was a primary Puritan concern that a minister had to be learned, and also godly in his behavior.
William Gurnall expressed the importance of these
qualities in his memorable statement: "Unholiness
in a preacher's life will either stop his mouth from
reproving, or the people's ears from receiving."

It was written of "Puritan" Scotland, just before the restoration of Charles II, that:

> Every minister was a very full professor of the
> reformed religion. . . . Every minister was obliged
> to preach thrice a week, to lecture and catechize
> once, besides other private duties wherein they
> abounded. . . . None of them might be scandal-
> ous in their conversation, or negligent in their
> office, so long as a presbytery stood.

Beyond everything else, the Puritans knew only too
well what the apostles had told members of the early
Church in Jerusalem: *"But we will give ourselves
continually to prayer, and to the ministry of the word"*
(Acts 6:4).

It was Froude, not a Puritan himself, who said: "It would have fared ill with England, had there been no hotter blood there that filtered in the sluggish veins of the officials of the Establishment." And he added that it was the young Puritans, in the heat and glow of their convictions, "who saved the Church which attempted to disown them."

On this matter of unworthy and ineffective clergy, it is very easy to prove that Shakespeare stood with the Puritans.

❖ ❖ ❖ ❖ ❖

By reading his plays, one has to agree with an author of many, many years ago, when he wrote that "Shakespeare was not a Papist, and it must be borne in mind that the evidence in proof thereof is given by himself — a testimony more powerful than the arguments of commentators."

Perhaps the strongest anti-papal statements are found in the play *King John*. King John reigned in England in the early part of the thirteenth century, and most Tudor historians emphasize the two most outstanding things in his career as being his signing of the *Magna Carta,* and *his defiance of the pope.* He is often seen as a sort of proto-Protestant.

In the play *King John*, we find the pope's legate, Cardinal Pandulph, addressing King John. (King Philip of France is also present).

Hail, you anointed deputies of heaven!
To thee, King John, my holy errand is.
I Pandulph, of fair Milan cardinal,
And from Pope Innocent the legate here,

Do in his name religiously demand
Why thou against the church, our holy mother,
So wilfully dost spurn; and force perforce
Keep Stephen Langton, chosen archbishop
Of Canterbury, from that holy see:

King John answers him:

What earthly name to interrogatories
Can taste the free breath of a sacred king?
Thou canst not, cardinal, devise a name
So slight, unworthy and ridiculous.
To charge me to an answer, as the pope,
Tell him this tale; and from the mouth of England
Add thus much more, that no Italian priest
Shall tithe or toil in our dominions;

....

So tell the pope, all reverence set apart
To him and his usurp'd authority.

King Philip tells King John: *"Brother of England, you blaspheme in this."* King John's response prognosticated the fury of Martin Luther by three hundred years:

Though you and all the kings of Christendom
Are led so grossly by this meddling priest,
Dreading the curse that money may buy out;
And by the merit of vild gold, dross, dust,
Purchase corrupted pardon of a man,
Who in that sale sells pardon from himself;
Though you and all the rest so grossly led
This juggling witchcraft with revenue cherish,
Yet I alone, alone do me oppose
Against the pope, and count his friends my foes.

Cardinal Pandulph answers the king and says: *"Then, by the lawful power that I have, Thou shalt stand curs'd and excommunicate."*

❖ ❖ ❖ ❖ ❖

We find a similar blast against the Roman priesthood in the play *King Henry VI*, Part 1. In it we find the Duke of Gloucester in much contention with the Bishop of Winchester, afterward Cardinal. The Duke of Gloucester, uncle to the king and Protector, is standing at the gates of the Tower. He finds the bishop (Winchester) there, and asks if he is trying to shut him out. The bishop answers: *"I do, thou most usurping proditor, And not Protector, of the king or realm."*

Gloucester answers:

> *Stand back, thou manifest conspirator,*
> *Thou that contrived'st to murder our dear lord,*
> *Thou that giv'st whores indulgences to sin:*
> *I'll canvas thee in thy broad cardinal's hat,*
> *If thou proceed in this thy insolence.*

At that time, the public brothels in Southwalk were under the jurisdiction of the Bishop of Winchester. The Duke of Gloucester knew that, and knew from the court books of the fees that were paid by the brothel keepers that the church reaped some of the benefits. The bishop is firm:

> *Nay, stand thou back; I will not budge a foot:*
> *This be Damascus, be thou cursed Cain,*
> *To slay thy brother Abel, if thou wilt.*

GLOUCESTER: *I will not slay thee, but I'll drive*
  thee back.
Thy scarlet robes, as a child' bearing-cloth,
I'll use to carry thee out of this place.
....
Under my feet I'll stamp thy cardinal's hat;
In spite of Pope or dignities of church
Here by the cheeks I'll drag thee up and down.

BISHOP: *Gloucester, thou'lt answer this before*
  the Pope.

GLOUCESTER: *Winchester goose! I cry, 'A rope*
  a rope!
Now beat them hence; why do you let them stay?
Thee I'll chase hence; why do you let them stay?
Thee I'll chase hence, thou wolf in sheep's array.
Out, tawny coats! Out, scarlet hypocrite!

Today, those words of the Duke of Gloucester do not convey the same menacing meaning as they did in Shakespeare's day. At that time it was a horrid and terrible insult, both to the bishop and to the church. *"Winchester goose"* meant a particular stage of a venereal disease contracted in the brothels. No epithet could have been more derisive to the *Bishop of Winchester.* Rarely would one find in print such scorn heaped on the clergy of the church.

❖ ❖ ❖ ❖ ❖

There are many other instances in Shakespeare's plays that would make some people believe that it must have been Shakespeare's own attitude toward the papacy and the priests of Rome. It certainly represented the Puritan attitude.

Shakespeare could well have agreed with the argument of Francis Bacon, that one reason for the growth of atheism was the scandals that existed appertaining to the priests. The priests are certainly the target in many of Shakespeare's plays. We will add just a few more to the two already given.

In the play *King Henry VI*, Part 2, the Earl of Salisbury, referring to Cardinal Beaufort, says:

> *Oft have I seen the haughty Cardinal*
> *More like a soldier than a man o' the church,*
> *As stout and proud as he were lord of all,*
> *Swear like a ruffian . . .*

In the same play, when the cardinal was on his deathbed, Vaux speaks to the queen, telling her:

> *Cardinal Beaufort is at point of death;*
> *For suddenly a grievous sickness took him,*
> *That makes him gasp, and stare, and catch the*
>   *air,*
> *Blaspheming God, and cursing men on earth.*

A little later, the cardinal speaks — for the last time: *"Give me some drink; and bid the apothecary bring the strong poison that I bought of him."* Rather than dying like a man of God, the cardinal dies more like an infidel, determined to commit suicide.

❖ ❖ ❖ ❖ ❖

In the play *King Henry VIII*, probably the most religious character to appear is Queen Katherine. She was the king's wife, but later divorced and banished to Kimbolton. When told that two cardinals

(Campeius and the famous Wolsey) requested to see her, she knew it was concerning the king's request to the pope for a royal divorce. At that point she said: *"They should be good men, their affairs as righteous: But all hoods make not monks."*

When the two cardinals came in and spoke to her, Queen Katherine addressed them: *"My lords, I thank you both for your good wills, Ye speak like honest men (pray God ye prove so)."*

Later, when the cardinals advised her to put her case in the king's care, she answered:

> *Ye tell me what ye wish for both, my ruin:*
> *Is this your Christian counsel? Out upon ye.*
> *Heaven is above all yet; there sits a judge*
> *That no king can corrupt.*

Cardinal Campeius tells her: *"Your rage mistakes us."* Queen Katherine responds:

> *The more shame for ye; holy men I thought ye,*
> *Upon my soul two reverend cardinal virtues:*
> *But cardinal sins and hollow hearts I fear ye.*

❖ ❖ ❖ ❖ ❖

In *Hamlet*, we find Ophelia telling Laertes:

> *Do not as some ungracious pastors do,*
> *Show me the steep and thorny way to heaven,*
> *Whiles like a puff'd and reckless libertine*
> *Himself the primrose path of dalliance treads.*

❖ ❖ ❖ ❖ ❖

In *Pericles,* we find the First Fisherman telling Pericles about a whale at sea, who "plays and tumbles, driving the poor fry before him, and at last devours them all at a mouthful." Then he adds:

> *Such whales have I heard on a'th' land, who never leave gaping till they swallow'd the whole parish, church, steeple, bells, and all.*

Pericles responds: *"A pretty moral."*

❖ ❖ ❖ ❖ ❖

In *Twelfth Night,* there is a caustic reference to the way some of the priesthood engaged in pretension and deception as they fulfilled their ministry. One of the accusations often made against Puritan ministers was that they refused to dissemble. Thomas Carter tells us that if the Puritan pastors had only cooperated in that sense, peace would have prevailed. He tells us in his book *Shakespeare and Holy Scripture,* "the Puritan steadfastly refused, and the utmost scorn was expressed against those men who were pitchforked into benefices or held their living by abject conformity." The clown in this play is obviously responding in the way that any good Puritan would do.

In the play, Maria tells the clown to act like a dissembling curate, put on a cassock, etc.

> *Nay, I prithee put on this gown, and this beard;*
> *Make him believe thou art Sir Topas the curate;*
> *do it Quickly. I'll call Sir Toby the whilst.*

Clown answers:

Well, I'll put it on, and I will dissemble myself in't, And I would I were the first that ever dissembled in such a gown. I am not tall enough to become the function well, Nor lean enough to be thought a good student; but to be said an honest man and a good housekeeper goes as fairly as to say a careful man and a great scholar.

❖ ❖ ❖ ❖ ❖

There was another important difference between Puritans and Catholics regarding places of worship. The Puritans agreed with James Ussher, the Anglican/Puritan Archbishop of Armagh, who told them: "In times of persecution the Godly did often meet in barns and such obscure places, which were indeed public because of the Church of God there; as wherever the prince is, there is the court." In addition, the Puritans believed that the trappings of ceremonies and outward adornment only hindered men from hearing the voice of God. And, of course, all the Puritans knew the words of Jesus on the matter. They found it in their Bible: "Ye fools and blind: for whether is greater, the gold, or the temple that sanctifieth the gold?" (Matt. 23:17). The ceremonies were certainly repugnant to the Puritans. Thomas Watson said: "Posture in worship is too often imposture." And Richard Greenham said in a similar vein: "The more ceremonies, the less truth."

This comes out very clearly in the play *Troilus and Cressida.* Hector tells his brother: *"'Tis mad idolatry to make the service greater than the god."*

❖ ❖ ❖ ❖ ❖

Such was the Puritan preaching that raged in England in those days. Many of them had read the books of the Puritan exiles like John Bale. He had written a book whilst in exile in Zurich, under the title *Yet a Course at the Romish Fox.* He condemned the ceremonies and rituals practiced in the Roman Catholic churches, considering them "doctrines of men, beggarly traditions, and dirty dregs of the pope."

Bale reminded them that Jesus never allowed such services. Jesus

> ... never went procession with cope, cross, and candlesticks. . . . He never hallowed church of chalice, ashes nor palms, candles nor bells. He never made holy water nor holy bread. . . . These mitres, tippets, furred amises, and shaven crowns . . . these matinses, masses, ceremonies, sorceries, shall not he know for his.

Later, Bale did modify some of his statements, telling the Puritan preachers that certain New Testament rites could be observed, especially baptism and the Lord's Supper. These, he told them, had the express command of God. Ceremonies not commanded by God should be removed altogether. That was the position of most Puritans for many generations after Bale.

The Puritan preachers proclaimed their doctrines with vigor, and crowds of people flocked to hear them.

It was obvious throughout England that the Puritans were determined to purge their worship of all Roman Catholic accretions, and restore biblical simplicity. A study of Puritan vocabulary has shown that *"naked"* was one of their positive words when applied to worship. In the Puritan church, the individual worshipper stood *naked* before the light and purity of God's Word and presence. Their buildings were such that one could hear God's Word without any distractions.

One author has stated that Puritan worship resembled the plays of Shakespeare, because they were content with the scantiest of stage props. Scenery and imagery were built into the plays themselves. In a similar way, the Puritans got rid of the stage scenery of Roman Catholic and Episcopalian worship, and relied instead on verbal imagery based on the Bible. The central place in the Puritan church was given to the *pulpit,* not to exalt the preacher, but instead to exalt the *Word of God.* In the pulpit, prominently enthroned on its pulpit cushion, was the Puritan Bible — a witness to its authority in the church.

Puritan Doctrines in Shakespeare's Plays

7 It would be wrong to assume that Shakespeare was a great theologian of the Church. That he was not. However, it would be equally wrong to assume that he was totally ignorant of the doctrines of the Church. As a matter of fact, he was far more knowledgeable in the cardinal doctrines of the Church than most people, including some of the clergy themselves. Shakespeare was equally knowledgeable in the doctrines that characterized the Puritans, and we will pay special attention to these as we study his plays.

In 1559, five years before Shakespeare was born, Queen Elizabeth I of England issued an ordinance forbidding any person, particularly playwrights and actors, to "abuse the Common Prayer in any interlude or Play." Shakespeare normally conformed with the established law of the land, but on this matter he may not have always kept the letter of the law. Whilst Shakespeare himself may have kept it, some of the characters in his plays certainly did not.

Anyone reading Shakespeare's plays would have

no difficulty in concluding that some of them had characters expressing various religious beliefs and biases, orthodox doctrines, and unorthodox. This, of course, is understandable, since a playwright has to make sure that his characters are credible. Expression has to be given to conflicting viewpoints, lifestyles, moral values, and religious suppositions. Each character is different. Some have concluded that because Shakespeare allowed some of his *dramatis personae* to participate in profane and imprecatory language, then he himself, as the author, had to be an irreligious person. This is not so. We have to remember, in the first place, that authors in Shakespeare's day did not have to express their own personal opinions to the media, as they do today. At that time, reticence was one of the marks of nobility. Also, a playwright then, as now, had to see to it that if there was a corrupt character in his play, the character's language had to correspond. This is not always an easy thing for an author to do, unless he knows personally a person who does live and speak in that particular way. If he doesn't, then he has to resort to some history book, hoping to find one.

Shakespeare, however, knew of another venue as well. From his wide knowledge of the Bible, he knew exactly where he could be furnished with an appropriate example. Here is one such example:

In his play *King Henry VI*, Part 3, England, not for the first time, experienced a struggle for the throne. Right at the end of the play, we find the sinister figure of Richard, Duke of Gloucester, a brother to the new king, appear on the stage. His brother George, Duke of Clarence, is also present. The new king, Edward IV, tells the two brothers: *"Clarence* and Gloucester, love my lovely Queen, And kiss your princely nephew, brothers both."

Clarence kisses the king's baby son, and is thanked by the queen. Richard then speaks: "And, that I love the tree from whence thou sprag'st, Witness the loving kiss I give the fruit."

Then as an aside, Richard says: "To say the truth, so Judas kiss'd his master and cried 'All hail' when as he meant all harm."

Where else could Shakespeare have been furnished with that concept, except in the story of Judas Iscariot in the Bible. There is no account, anywhere in human history, that portrays treachery and betrayal comparable to that seen in the Garden of Gethsemane. Shakespeare had only to read Matthew 26:48–49.

> Now he that betrayed him gave them a sign, saying, Whomsoever I shall kiss, that same is he: hold him fast. And forthwith he came to Jesus, and said, Hail, master; and kissed him.

As stated previously, Shakespeare had a phenomenal knowledge of the Scriptures, and the biblical quotations found in his plays are endless. However, there is another factor which convinces many scholars as they study his plays. Not only did Shakespeare know the words of Scripture, but he also had a profound understanding of the doctrinal truths they conveyed. As Shakespeare wrote himself: "The devil can cite Scripture for his purpose" (The Merchant of Venice). The mere words of Scripture, although an inspiration in themselves, would still be insufficient unless Shakespeare's purpose was to convey the Divine truth that they represented. The more one reads his plays, the more one realizes that Shakespeare's philosophy was to exalt the Divine message implied in the words. His dramas are saturated with doctrines.

❖ ❖ ❖ ❖ ❖

We will refer to some of the prominent Puritan doctrines that seem to emerge in some of his plays.

The doctrine of Human Depravity

This was a doctrine that the Puritans had learned in the schools of John Calvin. It was one of the five major points of Calvinism: total depravity. And where did Calvin learn the doctrine? The Puritans would have no difficulty in answering: **The Bible.** And where did Shakespeare learn about it? In the Puritan Bible, with its comprehensive Calvinistic notes.

Many critics have wondered why Shakespeare should have been so interested in the sinful nature of human beings. In play after play, one is introduced to the evil propensities of men and women. Was Shakespeare himself like this? Some of his critics seem to think so! One thing is crystal clear: Shakespeare certainly believed in human depravity. The noted literary historian Henry Hallam expressed it in this way:

> There seems to have been a period in Shakespeare's life when his heart was ill at ease, and ill content with the world or his own conscience; the memory of hours misspent, the pang of affection misplaced or unrequited, the experience of man's worser nature, which intercourse with ill chosen associates, by choice or circumstance,

peculiarly teaches. These, as they sank down into the depths of his great mind, seem only to have inspired it with the conception of Lear and Timon, but that of one primary character — *the censurer of mankind.*

Many people would have to agree with Hallam because it is a fact that becomes apparent in play after play. However, more people would agree if Hallam had added another reason. To be a censurer of mankind follows naturally from the doctrine of human depravity, which was at the core of the Puritan faith. Man, because of his sinful nature, was not only under the censure of God, but under His condemnation as well. Right at the beginning, God declared in Genesis 8:21, "the imagination of man's heart is evil from his youth." We find the same message in:

Timon of Athens:
all's oblique;
There's nothing level in our cursed natures
But direct villainy.

Othello:
guiltiness will speak
Though tongues were out of use.

Romeo and Juliet:
And where the worser is predominant
Full soon the canker death eats up that plant.

The Merchant of Venice:
Mark you this Bassanio,
The devil can cite Scripture for his purpose,

An evil soul producing holy witness
Is like a villain with a smiling cheek,
A goodly apple rotten at the heart,
O what a goodly outside falsehood has.

Measure for Measure:

Our natures do pursue
(Like rats that ravin down their proper bane)
A thirsty evil, and when we drink, we die.

Hamlet:

We are arrant knaves, all.

King Henry V:

Now if these men have defeated the law, and out-
run native punishment, though they can outstrip
men they have no wings to fly from God.

Hamlet:

In the corrupted currents of this world,
Offence's gilded hand may shove by justice;
And oft 'tis seen, the wicked prize itself
Buys out the law: But 'tis not so above:
There is no shuffling — there the action lies
In his true nature; and we ourselves compell'd,
Even to the teeth and forehead of our faults,
To give in evidence.

❖ ❖ ❖ ❖ ❖

The doctrine of Repentance

Man's sin and depravity is such that God asks man
to **repent** and to turn away from wicked and evil
ways. As He promised to Israel: "If that nation,

against whom I have pronounced, turn from their evil, I will repent of the evil that I thought to do unto them" (Jeremiah 18:8). The same call comes in the New Testament: ". . . except ye repent, ye shall all likewise perish" (Luke 13:3).

Two Gentlemen of Verona:

PROTEUS: My shame and guilt confounds me.
Forgive me, Valentine: if hearty sorrow
Be a sufficient ransom for offense,
I tender't here: I do as truly suffer.
As e'er I did commit.

VALENTINE: Then I am paid:
And once again I do receive the honest.
Who by repentance is not satisfied,
Is nor of heaven, nor earth; for these are pleas'd:
By penitence th' Eternal's wrath's appeas'd.

❖ ❖ ❖ ❖ ❖

The Taming of the Shrew:

Now Lord be thanked for my good amends.

This reminds us immediately of what the Bible states: "And he shall make amends for the harm that he hath done . . ." (Leviticus 5:16).

❖ ❖ ❖ ❖ ❖

The doctrine of the Atonement

Shakespeare not only knew the laws that came down from the queen of England, but knew as well, if not better, the laws that came down from the King of

—103—

kings. He knew that man had transgressed the Laws of his Maker, and that there was a price to pay. But he knew also that the God who punished the guilty is the same God who supplied a Redeemer. A ransom had been paid.

King Richard II:

> *. . . the world's ransom, blessed Mary's Son.*

The ransom being paid, the believer is now delivered from the curse of the Law.

King Henry VI, Part 2:

> *As surely as my soul intends to live*
> *With that dread King that took our state upon*
>   *Him*
> *To free us from his Father's wrathful curse*

The doctrine is even clearer as Isabella pleads for her brother's life in **Measure for Measure**.

> *ANGELO, THE DEPUTY OF VIENNA:*
> *He's sentenc'd, 'tis too late*
> ....
> *Your brother is a forfeit of the law,*
> *And you but waste your words.*

> *ISABELLA: Alas, alas!*
> *Why, all the souls that were, were forfeit once,*
> *And He that might the vantage best have took*
> *Found out the remedy. How would you be*
> *If He, which is the top of judgment, should*
> *But judge you as you are? O, think on that,*
> *And mercy then will breathe within your lips,*
> *Like man new made.*

Anybody living in England at that time who knew the history of the Crusades would fully understand what the king is referring to in the play *King Henry IV*, Part 1:

> *To chase these pagans in those holy fields*
> *Over whose acres walk'd those blessed feet*
> *Which fourteen hundred years ago were nail'd*
> *For our advantage on the bitter cross.*

❖ ❖ ❖ ❖ ❖

Another of the attributes of God was His **mercy.** The One who declares Himself a jealous God "visiting the iniquity of the fathers unto the third and fourth generation," also declares Himself a God whose "mercy endureth unto all generations."

The Merchant of Venice:

> *The quality of mercy is not strain'd,*
> *It droppeth as the gentle rain from heaven*
> *Upon the place beneath: it is twice blest,*
> *It blesseth him that gives, and him that takes,*
> *'Tis mightiest in the mightiest, it becomes*
> *The throned monarch better than his crown.*
> *His sceptre shows the force of temporal power,*
> *The attribute to awe and majesty,*
> *Wherein doth sit the dread and fear of kings:*
> *But mercy is above this sceptred sway,*
> *It is enthroned in the hearts of kings,*
> *It is an attribute to God himself;*
> ....
> *Therefore Jew,*
> *Though justice be thy plea, consider this,*

That in the course of justice, none of us
Should see salvation: we do pray for mercy,
And that same prayer, doth teach us all to render
The deeds of mercy.

Rarely does one hear on the stage today, or anywhere in our modern media, film, and press, such eminent doctrines of the Christian faith expressed with such sublimity.

❖ ❖ ❖ ❖ ❖

A prominent Puritan doctrine was that of **justification by faith.** This doctrine was one of the major reasons for the Protestant Reformation, initiated by Martin Luther. The Roman Catholic Church taught that justification was by *good works* and *human merit.* The Protestants, followed by the Puritans, taught that justification was *by grace through faith.*

Initially what triggered the whole Reformation movement in Europe was the system of indulgences practiced by the Roman Catholic Church. By its action the Catholic church was recognizing one of the commonest instincts of a human being, the natural desire to make amends for unworthy conduct. In that sense the Catholic church is very human, and many claim that to be its strength. The system of indulgences was an old practice of the church, going back to the thirteenth century. Its roots were even prior to that, when men were excommunicated from the church for certain sins. To be accepted back into membership required a public confession, plus certain satisfactions, like a substantial gift to the church, alms giving, freeing slaves, etc. With the process of time, the whole system was abused, and soon archbishops and bishops were allowed to dispense indulgences. Indulgences were soon being sold, and much of the money collected helped to build some of the medieval churches.

The final granting of indulgences was confined to the pope. Many indulgences were granted during the Crusades, with those participating being released from all kinds of penances, some even promised release from Purgatory.

Owing to satisfactions made by good men, there was a surplus of good deeds at the disposal of the pope. It was referred to as *Thesaurus Merit Orum.* *(The Treasury of Merit).* As time went on, the pope had a large pool to draw from, and soon he was able to designate to some churches the privilege of dispensing indulgences. The Castle Church in Wittenburg was one of them. It was at this church that Martin Luther nailed his ninety-five theses to the church door, and by so doing kindled the mightiest religious explosion ever in Europe.

It was this doctrine of justification, not by works but by faith, taught by Luther, developed even further by Calvin, that was now being preached vigorously by the Puritans in England. They felt that the Anglican/Episcopalian Church had not been sufficiently reformed, and the Puritans gained much of their momentum from the doctrines of John Calvin in Geneva.

Love's Labour's Lost:

See, see! my beauty will be saved by merit,
O heresy in fair, fit for these days!

King Henry IV, Part 1:

*O, if men were to be saved by merit, what hole in
Hell were hot enough for him?*

As before, Shakespeare was allowing one of his
dramatis personae to express the Puritan doctrine
that justification is by faith in God and not by human merit. Being well versed in the Bible, he knew
Paul's Letter to the Romans 3:28: "Therefore we
conclude that *a man is justified by faith without the
deeds of the law.*"

❖ ❖ ❖ ❖ ❖

On the subject of **grace,** besides the doctrine, there
is another interesting statement in *Hamlet:* "*A
double blessing is a double grace.*"

As today, so in the days of Shakespeare, when
we say a prayer before a meal, we sometimes call it
grace, sometimes blessing. It is very probable here
that Shakespeare had a verse in mind from the Apocrypha. In Ecclesiasticus 26:15 it reads: "A shamefast
and faithful woman is *a double grace.*"

Thomas Carter found an interesting reference
in Isaiah 40:2, where the prophet tells the people
the message from God:

> Speak ye comfortably to Jerusalem, and cry unto
> her, that her warfare is accomplished, that her
> iniquity is pardoned: for she hath received of the
> LORD's hand *double for all her sins.*

In the margin of the Geneva Version, it says : "*Sufficient or double grace whereas she deserved double
punishment.*" And an interesting comment follows:

This was fully accomplished when John the Baptist brought tidings of Jesus Christ's coming, who was the true deliverer of His Church from sin and Satan; hence the *double blessing of the Forerunner and the Messiah announced the sufficient or double grace of the forgiveness of God.*

❖ ❖ ❖ ❖ ❖

Knowing his Bible so well, it was not difficult for Shakespeare to depict the strategies and subtleties of **Satan.** He was acquainted with what Paul had told the Corinthians, that Satan can transform himself "into an angel of light."

Love's Labour's Lost:

Devils soonest tempt, resembling spirits of light.

Timon of Athens:

When devils will their blackest sins put on,
They do suggest at first with heavenly shows.

Not only is his appearance deceptive, but his statements also. As John informs us in the Book of Revelation, he "deceiveth the whole world."

MacBeth:

But 'tis strange:
And oftentimes to win us to our harm,
The instruments of Darkness tell us truths;
Win us with honest trifles, to betray us
In deepest consequence.

Measure for Measure:

O cunning enemy, that, to catch a saint,
With saints dost bait thy hook! Most dangerous

Is that temptation that doth goad us on
To sin in loving virtue.

King Richard III:

But then I sigh, and, with a piece of Scripture,
Tell them that God bids us do good for evil;
And thus I clothe my naked villainy
With odd old ends stolen forth of Holy Writ,
And seem a saint, when most I play the devil.

The Merchant of Venice:

The world is still deceived with ornament
In law, what plea so tainted and corrupt,
 But being season'd with a gracious voice,
Obscures the show of evil ? In religion,
What damned error but some sober brow
Will bless it, and approve it with a text,
Hiding the grossness with fair ornament.

❖ ❖ ❖ ❖ ❖

The doctrine of Hell

The Puritan preachers were vocal on this subject,
as was Jonathan Edwards later, when he preached
his famous sermon, "Sinners in the hands of an an-
gry God." In Shakespeare's plays the fire of hell is
depicted in various ways. In *Titus Andronicus* it is
everlasting fire; in *King Henry IV* it is *everlasting
bonfire light.*

MacBeth:

But this place is too cold for Hell, I'll devil porter
it no further, I had thought to have let in some of
all professions, that go the primrose way to th'
everlasting bonfire.

All's Well That Ends Well:

> I am for the house with the narrow gate, which I
> take to be too little for pomp to enter; some that
> humble themselves may, but the many will be too
> chill and tender, and they'll be for the flow'ry way
> that leads to the broad gate and **the great fire.**

❖ ❖ ❖ ❖ ❖

The Puritan emphasis on **purity** and **chastity** is never better expressed than by Isabella in *Measure for Measure*. It seemed that Claudio's life could only be saved if his sister, Isabella, submitted to the lustful desires of Angelo, the supposedly sainted Lord Deputy of Vienna. Claudio tells her: *"Death is a fearful thing."* His sister replies: *"A shamed life is hateful."* Claudio pleads:

> *Sweet sister, let me live.*
> *What sin you do to save a brother's life,*
> *Nature dispenses with the deed so far*
> *That it becomes a virtue.*

This does not sway Isabella; her passion for purity and chastity is superior to her brother's request. With pent-up force she answers him:

> *O, you beast!*
> *O faithless coward! O dishonest wretch!*
> *Wilt thou be made a man out of my vice?*
> *Is't not a kind of incest, to take life*
> *From thine own sister's shame!*
> ....
> *I'll pray a thousand prayers for thy death,*
> *No word to save thee.*

William
Shakespeare
and
His Bible

This last quotation from *Measure for Measure* brings us appropriately to the subject of **prayer.** It would certainly be true to say that if any playwright was well-versed in the biblical principles of prayer, it would be Shakespeare.

We are aware that a few of the prayers heard in his plays tend to be irreverent, and even profane — sometimes hypocritical. That can be understood when we realize that those who uttered them were profane and hypocritical characters. One has to admit, however, that normally Shakespeare treats prayer as the greatest duty a man owes his Maker. Most of the prayers heard in his plays are esteemed and treated with due reverence. One author claims that in over one hundred instances, the use of prayer in Shakespeare's plays are proper and reverential.

Shakespeare, of course, was not alone in this. The works of Milton could be placed in the same category, and so would the works of Samuel Johnston. James Rees tells us that before Dr. Johnson sat down to write his *Rambler,* which was meant to instruct as well as to amuse, he asked for God's guidance. His prayer was:

Almighty God, the giver of all good things, without whose help all labour is ineffectual, and without whose grace all wisdom is folly; grant, I beseech Thee, that in my undertaking Thy Holy Spirit may not be withheld from me, but that I may promote Thy glory, and the salvation both of myself and others; grant this, O Lord, for the sake of Jesus Christ. Amen.

When it comes to Shakespeare, many of his plays reveal biblical admonitions regarding prayer. In the quotations that follow, it is evident that Shakespeare knew that:

❖ Prayers, at times, are inaccurately made, but that God in his mercy sees to it that our requests are not granted. James 4:3: "Ye ask, and receive not, because ye ask amiss. . . ."

Anthony and Cleopatra:

> *We, ignorant of ourselves,*
> *Beg often our own harms, which the wise powers*
> *Deny us for our good; so find we profit*
> *By losing of our prayers.*

❖ Prayers are often ineffective, as the Lord reminds us through the Psalmist of Israel. Psalm 66:18: "If I regard iniquity in my heart, the Lord will not hear me."

Troilus and Cressida:

> *The gods are deaf to hot and peevish vows;*
> *They are polluted offerings, more abhorr'd*
> *Than spotted livers in the sacrifice.*

❖ Should our prayers be heard by others? Matthew 6:6: ". . . when thou prayest enter into thy closet, and when thou hast shut thy door, pray to thy Father which is in secret. . . ."

Much Ado About Nothing:

> *MARGARET: I have many ill qualities.*
> *BALTHASAR: Which is one?*

MARGARET: I say my prayers aloud
BALTHASAR: I love you the better; the hearers
may cry Amen.

Some have chosen *silent prayers* on the basis of Matthew 6:6, others *uttered prayers* that people may hear and say "Amen," quoting 1 Corinthians 14:15–16. The Geneva Bible has an interesting note: "One uttered the prayers, and all the company answered, Amen."

❖ However multitudinous, prayers without integrity of character, are not heard in heaven. Isaiah 1:15: ". . . yea, when ye make many prayers, I will not hear: your hands are full of blood."

Hamlet:
Words, without thoughts never to heaven go.

❖ ❖ ❖ ❖ ❖

❖ Prayer is our sole comfort in affliction. James 5:13: "Is any among you afflicted? let him pray."

The Tempest:
And my ending is despair,
Unless I be reliev'd by prayer,
Which pierces so, that it assaults
Mercy itself, and frees all faults.

❖ ❖ ❖ ❖ ❖

❖ Prayer, not vengeance, is the way of the saints. Romans 12:19: "Dearly beloved, avenge not yourselves, but rather give place unto wrath: for it is written, Vengeance is mine; I will repay, saith the Lord."

King Richard II:

Put we our quarrel to the will of heaven,
Who, when they see the hours ripe on earth,
Will rain hot vengeance on offenders' heads.

MacBeth:

Are you so gospell'd,
To pray for this good man and for his issue,
Whose heavy hand hath bow'd you to the grave,
And beggar'd yours for ever?

❖ ❖ ❖ ❖ ❖

❖ In the whole Bible, one can think of only one evil prayer being granted. Psalm 106:15: "And he gave them their request; but sent leanness into their soul."

Cymbeline:

I'll write against them,
Detest them, curse them: yet 'tis greater skill
In a true hate, to pray they have their will:
The very devils cannot plague them better..

Antony and Cleopatra:

We, ignorant of ourselves,
Beg often our own harms, which the wise powers
Deny us for our good; so find we profit
By losing of our prayers.

❖ Prayer before battle. A reference is frequently made to *King Henry V,* considered by most a national hero, and a Christian king. Preceding the Battle of Agincourt, he tells the French Ambassador:

> *We are no tyrant but a Christian king,*
> *Unto whose grace our passion is as subject*
> *As are our wretches fetterd in our prisons.*

Later Henry V is heard praying on his knees: *"O God of battles, steel my soldiers' hearts; Possesse them not with fear."*

King Henry then tells his commanders:

> *. . . he which hath no stomach to this fight,*
> *Let him depart; his passport shall be made*
> *And crowns for convoy put into his purse.*
> *We would not die in that man's company*
> *That fears his fellowship to die with us.*

It is so reminiscent of Gideon in the Book of Judges: "Now therefore go to, proclaim in the ears of the people, saying, Whosoever is fearful and afraid, let him return and depart. . . ."

Then the king speaks of those who stay for the battle:

> *This day is called the feast of Crispian.*
> *He that outlives this day and comes safe home*
> *Will stand a-tiptoe when this day is named*
> *And rouse him at the name of Crispian.*
> *He that shall see this day and live old age*

Will yearly on the vigil feast his neighbours,
And say, 'Tomorrow is Saint Crispian.'
Then will he strip his sleeve and show his scars,
And say, 'These wounds I had on Crispian's day,'
Old men forget; yet shall all be forgot
But he'll remember, with advantages,
What feats he did that day

....

This story shall the good man teach his son,
And Crispin Crispian shall ne'er go by
From this day to the ending of the world
But we in it shall be remembered,
We few, we happy few, we band of brothers.

When later told that the battle had been won, the Battle of Agincourt, King Henry responds: *"Praised be God, and not our strength, for it!"*

Then comes Captain Fluellen (the English pronouncement of the Welsh *Llewelyn*) reminding the king of the victories of his ancestors, his grandfather and his great uncle — the Black Prince of Wales. Their victories also were on the battlefields of France. He then tells King Henry:

> *I care not who know it. I will confess it to all the world: I need not to be ashamed of your majesty, praised be God, so long as your majesty is an honest man.*

The king responds: *"God keep me so!"*

A little later, Captain Fluellen asks the king: *"Is it not lawful, an't please your majesty, to tell how many is killed?"*

The king answers: *"Yes, Captain, but with this acknowledgment, that God fought for us."*

Shakespeare when writing these speeches of Captain Fluellen, was no doubt reminiscing about his school days in Stratford. One of his schoolmasters there was the Welshman Thomas Jenkins.

❖ ❖ ❖ ❖ ❖

On the subject of prayer, who can forget the words of Macduff to Malcolm in the play, **MacBeth:**

> *Thy royal father*
> *Was a most sainted King: the Queen that bore thee,*
> *Oft'ner upon her knees than on her feet,*
> *Died every day she lived.*

One is immediately reminded of the apostle Paul telling the Corinthians: "I die daily."

❖ ❖ ❖ ❖ ❖

A fitting, closing doctrine would be that of **death and the hereafter.** In spite of the element of mystery that surrounds both, the Puritans believed strongly in the sovereignty of God, and that it is God, and God alone, who has the keys of the world to come. We only know in part, God knows the whole.

Hamlet:
> *'Tis common, all that lives must die,*
> *Passing through nature to eternity.*

King John:
> *He who commands a nation*
> *Hath no commandment o'er the pulse of life.*

Cymbeline:

> By medicine life may be prolonged, yet death
> Will seize the doctor too.

King Henry V:

> We are in God's hand.

All's Well That Ends Well:

> It is not so with Him that all things knows,
> As 'tis with us that square our shows;
> But most it is presumption in us when
> The help of heaven we count the act of men.

Romeo and Juliet:

> A greater power than we can contradict
> Hath thwarted our intents.

❖ ❖ ❖ ❖ ❖

These Divine references was one of the major differences between Shakespeare and some of the other London dramatists of his generation. Shakespeare, at heart, was a Christian, and it was inevitable that it should appear from time to time in his plays. G, Wilson Knight, writing about the plays of Christopher Marlowe, tells us that "Marlowe's tragic heroes are all ambitious materialists, and when they crash, the end." Those of Shakespeare's plays are totally different, the reason being, said Knight, that "Shakespeare is fundamentally Christian, Marlowe pagan."

What better example than that expressed by Hamlet:

Our indiscretion sometime serves us well
When our deep plots do pall, and that should teach
  us
There's a divinity that shapes our ends,
Rough-hew them how we will.

❖ ❖ ❖ ❖ ❖

A Fitting Doxology from *King Henry VI*, Part 2

God's goodness hath been great to thee:
Let never day nor night unhallow'd pass,
But still remember what the Lord hath done.

Puritan Trends and Practices in Shakespeare's Plays

8 It should not be forgotten that Puritanism, in the main, was a religious movement. That is why Christian doctrine played such a major role in a Puritan's life and work. Following Christian salvation came Christian sanctification. It was in that category that ethical and social questions became important, and policies determined.

We all know from Shakespeare's plays that his *dramatis personae* were of every hue imaginable. Some were involved with apparitions, ghosts, spirits, etc. Others believed in fate, chance, lucky and unlucky stars, etc. Others embraced various philosophies, viewpoints, and lifestyles.

In one of Shakespeare's most famous plays, *Hamlet,* there are many references to ghosts and apparitions, with different actors reacting to them in different ways. Horatio had no problem accepting phenomenal events of that kind, and was ready to believe everything he was told. Hamlet, on the other hand, was far more cautious, and took far more time to be convinced.

One author claims that "Shakespeare seems to have taken more pains to discredit his supernatural machinery than any other infidel author, Goethe or Byron, who as poets, had to use it." Even W. J. Birch, who denies any semblance of the Christian faith in Shakespeare, readily admits that when Shakespeare introduces ghosts, apparitions, superstitions, etc., into his plays, he renders the whole idea "more ridiculous than sublime." He then continues by admitting that "Shakespeare always deals in mockery with supernatural machinery, whilst, at the same time he employs moral truths strikingly, effectively, and profoundly."

It is true that in the play *Hamlet* we find the Prince of Denmark deciding to kill his uncle, the king. His father's ghost had finally convinced him that it was his uncle who had murdered his father. When Hamlet goes on his errand of revenge, he finds his uncle on his knees in prayer. He feels that to kill him now in prayer would be to send him not to hell but to heaven. This would not be revenge, but rewarding his uncle's crime!

> *Now might I do it pat, now he is praying.*
> *And now I'll do't. And so he goes to heaven.*
> *And so am I reveng'd ? That would be scann'd:*
> *A villain kills my father, and for that*
> *I, his sole son, do this same villain send*
> *To heaven.*

Dr. Johnson says of this: "This speech, in which Hamlet represented as a virtuous character, is not content with taking blood for blood, but contrived damnation for the man that he would punish, is too horrible to be read or to be uttered." Even with that statement, W. J. Birch says that Dr. Johnson "was tender on the subject, because he sincerely believed in the doctrine of hell." Birch himself believed that Shakespeare had to be an infidel to be the author "of one of the most savage and shocking sentiments on record."

Certainly the matter of ethics and morality play a major role in *Hamlet,* and however savage and shocking was that statement of Shakespeare, we also know that in that same play, it was the same author who told us: *"There's a divinity that shapes our ends, rough-hew them as we will."*

Some of the terms used by Shakespeare in that statement may not be too clear to a modern-day reader. However, those terms are still being used on the farms surrounding Stratford even today. They still work in twos, cutting and trimming the hedges, and with the same language as fresh on their tongues as it was on Shakespeare's four hundred years ago! One *rough-hews* them, and the other *shapes their ends.*

Those who claim that Shakespeare was an infidel, attributing everything to Fate or Chance, would find his statement that it is God who shapes our ends, problematic. One critic tried to explain it by saying that Shakespeare here had changed his position "in deference to public opinion."

As stated previously, one must not forget that Shakespeare was a playwright with totally different personalities in his plays. Some would be pro-Christian, some anti-Christian. Some Catholic, some Episcopalian, some Puritans . . . some like Roderigo in *Othello* could be called a racist, and some in *The Merchant of Venice,* anti-Semitic. Being the author, Shakespeare had to supply a credible statement for all positions. Not all the characters would be able to share in the author's personal beliefs.

It is true that one finds some of the characters offensive, and some even profane. One must remember that such characters are depicting villains and boors, and their language fits their character. It does not mean that that was the way that Shakespeare himself spoke. As one author explained it: "Shakespeare's business was to imitate life, not to deliver sermons." Or in the words of Michael Macrone: ". . . his characters are his characters, not surrogate Shakespeare's."

Some, writing on Shakespeare, suggest that he had adopted the position of the schoolmen, men like Montaigne and Bacon. Their style was not to assume a definite position on any matter, but to argue both for and against. By taking such a middle-of-the-road attitude, they could never be accused of being orthodox or heretical.

That approach, however, did not apply to Shakespeare. He was not an essayist but a playwright. The characters he introduces often had strong opinions, and one knew exactly what they believed. Without that approach, the best of plays would be insipid.

Because Shakespeare's characters varied so much, so did his scriptural quotations. As we have already stated, he was so well versed in the Bible that he could always choose the right quotations for his characters. Thomas Carter wrote, over a century ago, that Shakespeare, in addition to knowing the

Bible, was also *daring* in quoting from it, so much so, that he was able "to dignify the thought of a king, to point the jest of a wit, or to brighten the dullness of a clown."

It is Thomas Carter who also reminds us that on the subject of apparitions, ghosts, and demons, Shakespeare got some of his material from a well-known Puritan book published at that time. It was written by Harsnett under the title *Declaration of Egregious Popish Impostures.* In his play *King Lear,* characters like Lear and Edgar use names and allusions obtained from this very book, especially concerning *demons of the earth and storm.*

❖ ❖ ❖ ❖ ❖

Some, at various times, have accused Shakespeare of being a *xenophobe.* It is true that certain nations and foreign groups did come under his literary lash. France and Spain would be typical examples.

As every historian knows, for a long time there had been constant conflict between them and England. Today we have the European Union, with France, Spain, and the United Kingdom members of it. There was no such union in Shakespeare's day. In those days, as we are reminded by Michael Macrone, it was "a condition exacerbated by their geographic insularity and their history of conflict with neighbors."

When some of Shakespeare's characters were accusative of the French, as in *King Henry V, Love's Labour's Lost,* and *Measure for Measure,* usually it was about some French social deportment or affection.

The Spanish would not be disparaged quite so often, and for something totally different. In all of Shakespeare's plays it is said that there was only one character who was truly a Spaniard. He was Don Armado in *Love's Labour's Lost.* To the citizens of England, his very name reminded them of the Spanish *Armada!* Shakespeare himself was old enough to recall the defeat of the Spanish Armada in 1588. It was only a few years later that he was writing his play *Love's Labour's Lost.*

It would be of greater interest for the purpose of this book to know the reason for Shakespeare's satire and invective of some other nations, particularly the *Turks.* This occurs in a number of plays, like *Othello, King Richard II, A Midsummer Night's Dream,* and *As You Like It.* Here are a few examples:

In *As You Like It,* Rosalind is referring to a very cruel letter written by Phebe:

> *Why, 'tis a boisterous and a cruel style,*
> *A style for challengers. Why, she defies me,*
> **Like Turk to Christian.**

In *King Richard II,* when Prince Hal became King Henry V of England, he assured everyone, including his opponents, that his rule would be moral and ethical, adding: *"This is the English, not the Turkish court."* They knew that some Turkish sultans, when they succeeded their father to the throne, would arrange for their brothers to be strangled.

What Prince Hal failed to mention was that his own father had succeeded to the throne of England by executing Richard II. It was at that time that the Bishop of Carlisle predicted that such a foul act would ultimately lead to a civil war.

And if you crown him, let me prophesy
The blood of English shall manure the ground,
And future ages groan for this foul act,
Peace shall go sleep with Turks and infi-
dels.

Why all these abusive slurs against the Turks? Once again we have to remind ourselves that Shakespeare had to portray exactly what he thought his characters believed. And Shakespeare well knew that it was not only the Bishop of Carlisle who considered the Turks to be heathens and infidels, but practically all in England, including Catholics, Episcopalians, and Puritans . . . they had never forgotten the Crusades! They knew, from their school days, the Turks' "long history of aggression against the Christian West" (Macrone).

In *MacBeth* we find one of the three witches saying: *"Nose of Turk, and Tartar's lips."* Here the Tartars are included with the Turks, both viewed as infidels, with the Tartars considered as "rough hearts of flints" as well. The Turks and the Tartars were related, and many in England associated their name *Tartars* with the Latin name *Tartarus,* meaning hell.

One should note that the word *Tartarus* is only found once in the whole Bible, and that in 2 Peter 2:4: "For if God spared not the angels that sinned, but cast them down to *hell* [Tartarus], and delivered them into chains of darkness, to be reserved unto judgment." Tartarus was a Greek word, and has been variously translated in our English versions.

❖ *The New English Bible:* "the dark pits of hell."

❖ *The New International Version:* "gloomy dungeons."

❖ Most other versions, simply: "hell."

Commentators often refer to it as a part of hell, having the distinctives of depth and darkness. One commentator defines it as "the vilest province of hell." Homer gave it the meaning of "subterranean." Most people, believing that Hades is the place where the spirits of the departed await the coming judgment, believe Tartarus to be a much darker and deeper abyss, reserved specially for the fallen angels.

One is reminded of the Puritan poet Milton:

And in the lowest deep, a lower deep
Still threatening to devour me opens wide.

❖ ❖ ❖ ❖ ❖

One of the great contributions of the Puritans was their emphasis on *liberty*. This they had learned in the school of Calvin. The famed American historian George Bancroft claimed regarding the Puritans that "the fanatic for Calvinism was a fanatic for liberty." And in our time, C. S. Lewis referred to the early Puritans as "young, fierce, progressive intellectuals, very fashionable and up-to-date."

All would agree that the Puritans were certainly *change agents*. That did not mean they were faultless, and Shakespeare knew that as well as anyone. He knew that they loved contention, and could be very argumentative, even regarding trivial matters. He had no doubt heard people criticize the Puritans for their desire for, and love of, filthy lucre, plus, at times, an eagerness for worldly power. According to one historian, they often scoffed at Greek learning for the simple reason that it was not Hebrew! And they liked playing with words, as indeed did Shakespeare himself. In one play of that period — not by Shakespeare — entitled *The Puritan,* a major theme of one of the characters was to make the distinction between *robbery* and *stealing!*

Shakespeare, however, different from most playwrights, understood the positive side of Puritanism. He knew full well the type of lifestyle the Puritans advocated. It was a life that fostered civility, dignity, sobriety, honesty, and purity, and above all else, a life with profound faith in God, and in the liberty of human conscience.

❖ ❖ ❖ ❖ ❖

Because of their strong stand on liberty, one can understand their concern for the *position of women in society.* This Puritan trait becomes apparent in many of Shakespeare's plays.

It is tragic how some modern-day critics have nearly convinced themselves, and others, that Shakespeare was well-nigh a misogynist. Harold Bloom, in his latest book on Shakespeare, assails such critics, referring to them as "the School of Resentment, the Feministas. . . ." Shakespeare was certainly in the Puritan tradition, emphasizing the liberty of women, totally different from the position advocated by many in the government and in the Established Church of his day. He knew full well that this position on liberty could be traced back to Martin Luther and the Reformation, and that it had been aggressively developed by the Puritans.

An example that is often given is that of Lady Anne during the Civil War in England. Her husband was Sir William Waller, one of the leaders of the Parliamentary army, and often referred to as *the Night Owl*. Lady Anne was the daughter of the Speaker of Parliament, the man who was "held down in his chair by Denzil Holles before the dissolution of the 1629 Parliament." In time, Lady Anne became as great a leader as her husband, and zealous in her Christian beliefs. Before she married her husband, she proposed that they should spend a day together in prayer to "seek God's blessing on their marriage."

She was the new type of Puritan woman, anxious to enter the world of their husbands. Some of them, like Lady Anne, played a major role in the life of their community. Some claim that Lady Anne once wanted to be the commander of her husband's army! She did not quite reach that pinnacle, but she certainly carried great influence as the general's wife.

Too often the Puritans were vilified on the subject of women, particularly regarding sex, marriage, and divorce. They were sometimes accused of being sexually inhibited and repressive. History, however, has proved that they were not nearly as sexless and bloodless as their critics imagined.

In one church in New England, a wife complained to her pastor, and then to the whole congregation, that her husband was neglecting their sex life. The Puritan church proceeded to excommunicate her husband.

Thomas Hooker, a noted Puritan, wrote:

The man whose heart is endeared to the woman he loves . . . dreams of her in the night, hath her

in his eye and apprehension when he awakes,
museth on her as he sits at the table, walks with
her when he travels. . . . She lies in his bosom
and his heart trusts in her.

One author described the Puritan marriage as a *"perfect sharing,"* and called it *"Puritanism's greatest and most admirable cultural achievement."* It is no wonder that the historian Green could claim: *"Home as we now conceive it, was the creation of the Puritan."*

Compared with other cultures, it could certainly be claimed that Puritanism gave women an elevated status. This no doubt evolved from their doctrine of the *priesthood of all believers,* and from the new role extended to women as consorts in a companionate marriage.

Probably the Puritan leaders would all have agreed with William Secker when he said that God made Eve a *"parallel line drawn equal to Adam,"* not created *"from his head to claim superiority, but out of the side to be content with equality."*

❖ ❖ ❖ ❖ ❖

Regarding the position of women in Shakespeare's plays, one could well begin with *As You Like It.* Toward the end of that play, Touchstone has a dialogue with Audrey, and tells her that tomorrow would be a very joyful day for them because tomorrow they are going to be married. In reply, Audrey tells him:

> *I do desire it with all my heart; and I hope it is
> no dishonest desire, to desire to be a woman of
> the world.*

Today, the expression *woman of the world* is often interpreted as *not* being a good wife at home. Rarely, if ever, is the expression used in a wedding ceremony. Why then should Shakespeare use it here? He was obviously reverting to a scriptural expression, as found in 1 Corinthians 7:34. In that verse, the apostle Paul explains the difference between a wife and a virgin. *A virgin "careth for the things of the Lord, that* she may be holy both in body and in spirit." *A married woman* on the other hand, says Paul, *"careth for the things of the world, how she may please her husband."*

In the play *The Taming of the Shrew*, Petruchio, referring to Kate says:

> *She is my goods, my chattels, she is my house,*
> *My household stuff, my field, my barn,*
> *My horse, my ox, my ass, my any thing,*
> *And here she stands. Touch her whoever dare!*

Shakespeare was no doubt remembering the Tenth Commandment, and applying it here to the importance of a woman in the household.

❖ ❖ ❖ ❖ ❖

Shakespeare, like all authors, knew that women differ greatly from each other. Some women were weak and frail, as Hamlet tells us: *"Frailty, thy name is woman."* In *As You Like It*, Rosalind uses a more biblical expression: *"But I must comfort the weaker vessel."*

In many of Shakespeare's plays, however, a woman is depicted with a far more liberated view of life. Maybe, for the first time in England, they saw in Shakespeare's plays the portrait of a Puritan girl. There are quite a number of them. A good example would be Cordelia in the play *King Lear.*

Cordelia was the youngest of the king's daughters, and the most pure and honest of the three. When King Lear decided to divide his kingdom between the three, he asked each for a statement of love. On receiving it, he would then determine what portion of the kingdom he would give each one as a dowry. The first daughter expressed her love by saying that she loved her father more than eyesight, space, liberty, even life itself. The second daughter gave a similar answer. The youngest daughter, Cordelia, gave quite a different answer. She confided to her father that her love for him could not be expressed; it was too weighty for her tongue to tell. Her love was in her heart, not in her mouth. She was willing to sacrifice eloquence for truth.

King Lear urged her to say more, then her dowry would be more opulent than that of her sisters. Asked what she could add to the statement she had already made, her answer was: *"Nothing my lord."*

LEAR: Nothing?

CORDELIA: Nothing.

LEAR: How, nothing will come of nothing. Speak again.

CORDELIA: Unhappy that I am, I cannot heave my heart into my mouth. I love your majesty according to my bond, no more nor less.

LEAR: How, how, Cordelia? Mend your speech a little, lest you may mar your fortunes.

CORDELIA: Good my lord, you have begot me, bred me, loved me. I return those duties back as are right fit. Obey you, love you, and most honour you. Why have my sisters husbands, if they say they love you all? Haply when I shall wed that lord whose hand must take my plight shall carry half my love with him, half my care and duty. Sure I shall never marry like my sisters "To love my father all."

King Lear then ordered that his kingdom be divided between the two other sisters. He told Cordelia that her *truth* should be her dowry.

In time, however, King Lear learned the hard way what the other two sisters meant by their love. He also realized how he had misunderstood and mistreated Cordelia, the only loyal and faithful one of the three.

We find in other plays of Shakespeare also, characters with similar traits to Cordelia. There was Rosalind in *As You Like It*. *"Do you not know I am a woman? When I think, I must speak."*

And Lucetta in *The Two Gentlemen of Verona:* *"I have no other but a woman's reason: I think him so, because I think him so."*

And others like Helena in *All's Well That Ends Well;* Isabella in *Measure for Measure;* Desdemona in *Othello*; Miranda in *The Tempest;* Hermione in *The Winter's Tale;* Imogen in *Cymbeline;* Marina in *Pericles,* etc. These were all educated women, and as John Adair writes, "girls of spirit."

They knew exactly what they wanted, and said so. They wanted to choose their own husbands, with their own rationale and emotions being recognized. Their number alone presents a salient case that Shakespeare knew the Puritan trend on liberty of conscience.

❖ ❖ ❖ ❖ ❖

Another subject that deserves attention is the way Shakespeare deals with the question of suicide, or as it is sometimes expressed in his plays: *self-slaughter.*

From the Christian standpoint, suicide has always been regarded as a mortal sin. Many Christians have put *self-murder* in the same category as murder, and leads to final severance from the forgiveness of God.

It has often been asked why so many of Shakespeare's characters should end up killing themselves. And perhaps in the plays *Julius Caesar* and *Antony and Cleopatra* more than any of the others. In the play *Julius Caesar,* we find Brutus, his wife Portia, as well as Cassius committing suicide. Portia kills herself off-stage. She had realized that the murder of Caesar, in which her husband had a prominent part, would soon make their life unbearable, if not impossible. Brutus tells Cassius how it happened:

> *Impatient of my absence,*
> *And grief that young Octavius with Mark Antony*
> *Have made themselves so strong, for with her death*
> *That tidings came. With this she fell distract,*
> *And, her attendants absent, swallow'd fire.*

Cassius, one of the other conspirators against Caesar, calls upon Pindarus, whose life he had once saved, to come and use the very sword with which he had killed Caesar, to kill him.

O, coward that I am, to live so long,
To see my best friend ta'en before my face!
....
Come hither, sirrah,
In Parthia did I take thee prisoner;
And then I swore thee, saving of thy life,
That whatsoever I did bid thee do,
Thou shouldst attempt it. Come now, keep thine
*   oath.*
Now be a freeman, and with this good sword,
That ran through Caesar's bowels, search this
*   bosom,*
Stand not to answer. Here, take thou the hilts,
And when my face is cover'd, as 'tis now,
Guide thou the sword. — Caesar, thou art
*   reveng'd,*
Even with the sword that kill'd thee. (Dies.)

Brutus, at the end of the play, turns to one of his staff that was still with him, Strato, and tells him:

I prithee, Strato, stay thou by thy lord,
....
Hold then my sword, and turn away thy face,
While I do run upon it. Wilt thou, Strato?

STRATO: *Give me your hand first. Fare you well,*
*   my lord.*

Brutus' last words:

Farewell, good Strato. — Caesar, now be still,
I kill'd not thee with half so good a will. (Dies.)

It is no wonder that Mark Antony referred to Brutus as "the noblest Roman of them all."

❖ ❖ ❖ ❖ ❖

In the play *Antony and Cleopatra*, five of the characters committed suicide: Eros, Mark Antony, Cleopatra, Charmian, and Iras.

Eros was one of Mark Antony's followers. He is asked by his master to take his sword and kill him. *"For with a wound I must be cured."* Eros hesitates, but Mark Antony insists.. Finally, Eros tells him:

My dear master,
My captain, and my emperor, let me say
Before I strike this bloody stroke, farewell.

ANTONY: 'Tis said, man, and farewell.

EROS: Farewell, great chief. Shall I strike now ?

ANTONY: Now, Eros.

EROS: Why, there then! (Kills himself)
Thus I do escape the sorrow
Of Antony's death.

Antony, when he saw that Eros had killed himself, says:

Thrice nobler than myself !
Thou teachest me, O valiant Eros, what
I should and thou couldst not !

Cleopatra, at the end of the play, applies an asp (a cobra of Egypt) to her breast:

> *Come, thou mortal wretch,*
> *With thy sharp teeth this knot intrinsicate*
> *Of life at once untie. Poor venomous fool,*
> *Be angry and dispatch.*

She tells Charmian, one of her attendants:

> *Peace, peace!*
> *Dost thou not see my baby at my breast*
> *That sucks the nurse asleep?*
> ....
> *As sweet as balm, as soft as air, as gentle —*
> *O Antony! — Nay, I will take thee too.*

Then Cleopatra applied another asp to her arm, and says: *"What should I stay"* — (Dies).

   Charmian — immediately following Cleopatra's self-inflicted death, a guard comes into the room asking for the queen. Charmian tells him to speak softly, and not to wake her. The guard replies that Caesar had sent him. Charmian answers: *"Too slow a messenger."* She then applies an asp to herself. *"O come apace! Dispatch! I partly feel thee."* When questioned again about the queen, Charmian answers:

> *It is well done, and fitting for a princess*
> *Descended of so many royal kings.*
> *Ah, soldier! (Charmian dies)*

Iras — like Charmian, Iras was an attendant to Cleopatra. She had been told what would happen, now that Caesar had the power:

CLEOPATRA: Now, Iras, what think'st thou?
Thou an Egyptian puppet shall be shown
In Rome as well as I. Mechanic slaves
With greasy aprons, rules and hammers shall
Uplift us to the view. In their thick breaths,
Rank of gross diet, shall we be enclouded
And forced to drink their vapour.

Iras answers: *"The gods forbid!"*

Iras' death is not explicitly told, but it happens just prior to that of Cleopatra and Charmian, in what could be termed a triple suicide.

❖ ❖ ❖ ❖ ❖

It is natural to ask: Why should there be so many suicides in these two plays? Was Shakespeare himself of the opinion that suicide was acceptable? Believing that Shakespeare was a Christian, and a Puritan Christian, the answer would have to be in the negative. There are two important things to remember:

First, in the two plays, *Julius Caesar* and *Antony and Cleopatra*, Shakespeare was dealing with Roman and Egyptian citizens who were living in a pre-Christian era. When Julius Caesar was in power in Rome, and Cleopatra in Egypt, Christ had not been born. It was a long time later that Rome became Christian, and the center of the Christian West.

Shakespeare, knowing his history, was dealing with a pagan world. In many of the pagan civilizations suicide was often considered not a disgrace, but a noble gesture. Even today, in some Far Eastern countries, people after an accident for which they may be partly responsible, often commit suicide. There is something perverse in a culture that acquiesces in, and often esteems, such action. This is totally unlike a Christian civilization, where suicide is referred to as a mortal sin. As Michael Macrone tells us: "Suicide is the devil's choice."

Second, when Shakespeare writes a play like *Hamlet,* the attention given to suicide is not the same. There we are told of Ophelia falling "in the weeping brook," and being drowned. It was a mystery then, and still is, whether it was suicide or an accident. In the play, the gravediggers are arguing how Ophelia should be buried. One of them asks: *"Is she to be buried in Christian burial, when she willfully seeks her own salvation?"*

Another gravedigger answers: *"I tell thee she is, therefore make her grave straight. The crowner hath sat on her and finds it Christian burial."*

In the same play, we have another reference to suicide, or as it is referred to in the play, self-slaughter. Hamlet, the Prince of Denmark, after a conversation with the king and queen, finds himself in a deep state of stress.

> *O that this too sullied flesh would melt,*
> *Thaw and resolve itself into a dew,*
> *Or that the Everlasting had not fix'd*
> *His canon 'gainst self-slaughter. O God! O God!*

Here Hamlet was desiring the annihilation of his own existence, but unfortunately God had expressed in the canon of Scripture that self-slaughter was forbidden.

Hamlet was not alone in this. In the play

Cymbeline, we find Imugen, the king's daughter, express the same desire. She also is restricted by a Divine prohibition.

> *Against self-slaughter*
> *There is a prohibition so divine*
> *That cravens my weak hand*

One critic, who denied that Shakespeare was a Christian, quoted the statement of Hamlet to prove that Shakespeare did not know his Bible very well; he claimed that there is not a verse in Scripture that tells of a Divine decree against suicide.

The critic may be correct that the word *suicide* or *self-slaughter* is not found in the Bible, but Shakespeare knew full well the Bible teaching on the subject. He knew that God's decree was specifically against a person killing himself. Suicide may be a means of escape from a sea of troubles and torments in this world, but never an escape from the anger of God in the world to come.

One of Shakespeare's favorite biblical books was that of Job; he quotes from it over forty times in his History Plays alone. It was also a favorite with many of the Puritan preachers. It is said that Joseph Caryl preached from the Book of Job every Sunday for twenty-four years! When he later published his commentary on Job, it came to twelve volumes, quarto size! In the Book of Job, Shakespeare would certainly have known 1:21: *"The LORD gave, and the LORD hath taken away; blessed be the name of the LORD."* And he would have known the sixth commandment in Exodus 20: *"Thou shalt not kill."* And from his knowledge of the New Testament, he would have

known 1 John 3:15: *". . . and ye know that no mur-
derer hath eternal life abiding in him."* Shakespeare
also knew of biblical personalities like King Saul in
the Old Testament, and Judas Iscariot in the New
Testament, who committed suicide, and knew that
neither of them was exonerated by God.

In the opinion of many, Shakespeare's most famous play was *Hamlet*. Harold Bloom, in his massive new book on Shakespeare, says of *Hamlet:*

> It is theater of the world, like The Divine Com-
> edy or Paradise Lost. . . . Hamlet remains apart,
> something transcendent about him places him
> more aptly with the Biblical King David, or even
> with more exalted scriptural figures . . . a charis-
> matic-of-charismatics.

He then adds a very pertinent comparison, that
Hamlet, like Job in the Old Testament, "is much
given to rhetorical questions."

A typical example of this in *Hamlet* would be on
this question of suicide. Those, who at some point
in life, who may have considered a *way out* from the
calamities that beset them, may well have read, and
re-read, these words of Hamlet:

> *To be, or not to be, that is the question:*
> *Whether 'tis nobler in the mind to suffer*
> *The slings and arrows of outrageous fortune,*
> *Or take to arms against a sea of troubles*
> *And by opposing end them. To die — to sleep,*
> *No more; and by a sleep to say we end*
> *The heart-ache and the thousand natural shocks*
> *That flesh is heir to: 'tis a consummation*

Devoutly to be wish'd. To die, to sleep;
To sleep, perchance to dream — aye, there's the
rub;
For in that sleep shuffled off this mortal coil,
Must give us pause

....

Who would fardels bear,
To grunt and sweat under a weary life,
But that the dread of something after death,
The undiscover'd country, from whose bourn
No traveller returns, puzzles the will,
And makes us rather bear those ills we have
Than fly to others that we know not of ?

❖   ❖   ❖   ❖   ❖

Shakespeare realized, as do most of us, that there are still unanswered questions in life, and that the half has not been told. However, in spite of that, he believed in the old Puritan doctrine, that in the final analysis: **God's will, will be.** It is Shakespeare's indomitable faith in the sovereignty of God that gives his works an eternal quality. Did anyone ever express it so sublimely, and yet so succinctly, as Shakespeare did in *Measure for Measure:*

The words of heaven; on whom it will, it will;
On whom it will not, so; yet still 'tis just.